Eyewitness
Assemblies

15 ready-to-use assemblies for Easter to Pentecost

Gaynor Cobb

For Laura

Acknowledgment

My thanks to Sue Doggett, not only for editing this book but also for her invaluable help in discussion and planning, which made this work such an enjoyable task. Thanks also to the staff and pupils at Wittersham Church of England School in Kent and St George's School, Windsor Castle.

Jesus said, 'Thomas, do you have faith because you have seen me? The people who have faith in me without seeing me are the ones who are really blessed!'
JOHN 20:29

Contents

Foreword

'Come and see,' said Philip to Nathanael, drawing him in to meet and experience Jesus, the Messiah. The most powerful stories in the Bible come from the spoken word, the personal account and, of course, the words and actions of Jesus.

Gaynor Cobb has captured the essence of the amazing stories in the build-up to Easter and the events leading to Pentecost. Vivid portrayals of personal dilemmas, marvellous insights and shared suffering are bound together in stories, reflections and role play that will engage and inform teachers and pupils alike.

I am very happy to commend the stories in this book to teachers and ministers anxious to make collective worship in our schools a living experience of Christ's love and sacrifice for us.

Easter is, of course, at the heart of the Christian year: so many things flow into and from this event. While the materials here will give special insights for the spring and summer seasonal terms in our schools, they range far wider than that in the subjects and issues they touch upon. Hence the very useful links with PSHE and Citizenship, alongside their relevance to the RE national framework, which is increasingly informing locally agreed RE syllabi around the country.

Everyone from the committed theologian to the newly qualified teacher will find sustenance and depth within these carefully crafted but biblically faithful eyewitness accounts of central events of the Christian story. Above all, the framework here will allow children themselves to find something special within the stories told and the roles they can play in making sense of those accounts.

In church and community schools up and down the land, this book will bring fresh expressions to the legally required and potentially inspiring act of collective worship that children still experience daily.

Rupert Bristow
Director of Education, Canterbury Diocese, and Chair of Kent SACRE

Introduction

Eyewitness Assemblies can be used to deliver whole-school, Key Stage or class assemblies during spring term, summer term or at other times of year to consider a variety of Christian themes. Each assembly can be used as a stand-alone at any time of the year, but the assemblies can also be used to form a series starting in the weeks before Easter and continuing after the Easter break. Teachers may also use the material as part of RE lessons, to help pupils gain an understanding of the events associated with the death and resurrection of Christ.

Each story is written in the first person, from the point of view of someone involved in the events.

The book covers aspects of Jesus' ministry, death and resurrection. Much of the material is centred on the events and personalities of the Easter story, but it also extends beyond Easter to include assemblies dealing with the resurrection appearances of Jesus, the ascension, Pentecost and the conversion of Paul on the road to Damascus.

Visual aids and introductory questions are suggested for each assembly, along with an introduction that may be read before the 'eyewitness story'. Poetry, news reports and drama ideas are also given. These may be performed by pupils to emphasize the message of the assembly. (When a poem is read, a candle may be lit in order to create an atmosphere of reflection. Many schools use candles during their time of worship.) Some of the ideas given may be useful for pupil performance in church celebrations.

Each section includes a prayer and suggestions for suitable songs. Suggested music could be used to top and tail the assembly.

The teacher's notes give curriculum links so that the assemblies may be followed up within the classroom. This could be of particular use where the assembly forms part of the RE syllabus.

Story synopsis for each assembly

1. Andrew's story is written from a disciple's point of view, describing Jesus' invitation to the fisherman to become a close friend of Jesus. The story helps to explain Jesus' ministry and, in particular, the miracle of raising Lazarus from the dead.

2. Judas' story tries to suggest how Judas felt when Jesus rode into Jerusalem, hailed as a king by cheering crowds who threw down palm leaves in front of him. The story attempts to set the scene for Judas' betrayal of Jesus.

3. Caiaphas' story explores the events in the temple when Jesus overturned the money changers' tables. It is written from the point of view of the chief priest and shows how the religious leaders plotted against Jesus.

4. Jesus' story uses words from John's Gospel to describe the preparations that Jesus made for his own death. During the last supper, Jesus washes his disciples' feet. He breaks the bread, takes wine and talks of the coming of the Holy Spirit. Jesus shows that he is aware of his impending betrayal by Judas.

5. Marcus' story describes the events in the garden of Gethsemane. It is written from the point of view of a soldier who realizes that the man who has been arrested is far from ordinary.

6. Peter's story (1) takes listeners to the night when Peter denied knowing Jesus three times before the cock crowed.

7. Pilate's story: the trial before Pilate is described by Pilate himself, explaining why he did not want Jesus to be executed.

8. The story of Good Friday is based on the poem 'Death', which describes the events of the crucifixion. It links the units leading

up to Easter with those beyond: the resurrection, the ascension, Pentecost and the early Church.

9. Mary Magdalene's story tells of Mary's feelings when she finds the empty tomb and then sees the risen Jesus, at first mistaking him for the gardener.

10. Cleopas' story takes listeners along the road to Emmaus, where two disciples encounter a stranger who is revealed to be Jesus.

11. Thomas' story investigates faith through Thomas' scepticism and his refusal to believe until he sees Jesus' wounds.

12. Peter's story (2) shows how Peter experienced Jesus' forgiveness and how he began his journey to establish the Christian Church.

13. Matthew's story describes Jesus' ascension to heaven through the eyes of those who loved him.

14. Philip's story deals with the coming of the Holy Spirit at Pentecost and the events that followed.

15. Paul's story investigates the powerful events that caused a man who persecuted the early Christians to encounter Jesus for himself and become a major influence in the spread of world-wide Christianity. (Paul changed his name from Saul to Paul after his conversion to Christianity.)

Framework links for RE, PSHE and Citizenship

Eyewitness assembly	RE Framework	PSHE and Citizenship National Curriculum KS2	QCA Unit for RE
Andrew's story	1a, b, e, f, g, h 2a, b, c, e 3e, f, h, i, j, k, o, p, q, r, s	1a, b, c, d, e 2e, h	3c, 3d, 3e 4c; 5d; 6c
Judas' story	1a, e, f, g, h 2b, c, d, e 3a, e, f, j, k, m, o, p, q, r, s	1a, b, d 2d, e	3c, 3d 4c
Caiaphas' story	1a, e, f, g, h 2b, c, d, e 3a, e, f, i, j, k, m, s	1a, b, c 2a, b, e, h	3c, 3d 4c 6a
Jesus' story	1a, b, c, e, f, g, h 2c, e 3f, g, h, i, j, k, p, q, r, s	1a, b, e 2a, d, e, h	3c, 3d, 3e 4c 6a, 6c, 6f
Marcus' story	1a, e, f, g, h 2c, d, e 3e, f, i, j, o, p, q, r	1a 2a, e	3c, 3d 4c
Peter's story (1)	1a, e, f, g, h 2b, c, d, e 3e, f, i, j, k, o, p, q, r	1a, b 2a, e, f	3c, 3d 4c 5d
Pilate's story	1a, b, e, f, g, h 2b, c, d, e 3e, f, h, i, j, k, o, p, q, r, s	1a, b, c 2a, e, f, k	3c, 3d 4c 6f
Good Friday's story	1a, b, c, e, f, g, h 2c, e 3e, f, h, i, j, o, p, q, r, s	1a, b 2a, e	3c, 3d 4c
Mary Magdalene's story	1a, b, c, e, f, g, h 2c, e 3e, f, g, h, i, j, k, o, p, q, r, s	1a 2a, e	3c, 3d, 3e 4c; 5d 6c, 6f
Cleopas' story	1a, b, c, e, f, g, h 2c, e 3e, f, g, h, i, j, k, o, p, q, r, s	1a, b, c, d 2a, e	3c, 3d, 3e 4c; 5d 6c, 6f
Thomas' story	1a, c, e, f, g, h 2a, b, c, e 3e, f, h, i, j, k, o, p, q, r, s	1a 2a, e, f	3c, 3d, 3e 4c 6f
Peter's story (2)	1a, b, e, f, g, h 2a, b, c, e 3e, f, h, i, j, k, o, p, q, r, s	1a, b, c, d 2a, e, f	3c, 3d, 3e 4c
Matthew's story	1a, b, e, f, g, h 2c, e 3e, f, g, h, i, j, o, p, q, r, s	1a 2a, e	3c, 3d, 3e 4c 6f
Philip's story	1a, b, d, e, f, g, h 2a, b, c, d, e 3e, f, g, h, i, j, k, o, p, q, r, s	1a, b, c 2a, e, k	3c, 3d, 3e 4c 6a, 6c, 6f
Paul's story	1a, f, g, h 2b, c, e 3e, f, h, i, j, k, o, p, q, r, s	1a, b, c 2a, e, f	3c, 3d, 3e 4c; 5d 6c

Andrew's story

The story of Lazarus is set in Bethany, but Andrew's eyewitness account also looks back to the time when Jesus first chose him to be one of his disciples and the life-changing events that followed.

The story can be used to retell one of Jesus' miracles or as part of an assembly about Jesus' disciples at any time of year. The story is followed by a reflective poem exploring the subject of faith.

Bible references

Jesus chooses Andrew

MARK 1:16–18

As Jesus was walking along the shore of Lake Galilee, he saw Simon and his brother Andrew. They were fishermen and were casting their nets into the lake. Jesus said to them, 'Come with me! I will teach you how to bring in people instead of fish.' At once the two brothers dropped their nets and went with him.

Jesus and the catch of fish

LUKE 5:1–11

Jesus told Simon, 'Don't be afraid! From now on you will bring in people instead of fish' (v. 10b).

Jesus and the death of Lazarus

JOHN 11:1–44

A man called Lazarus was sick in the village of Bethany. He had two sisters, Mary and Martha… The sisters sent a message to the Lord and told him that his good friend Lazarus was sick (vv. 1 and 3).

Jesus then said, 'I am the one who raises the dead to life! Everyone who has faith in me will live, even if they die. And everyone who lives because of faith in me will never really die' (vv. 25–26).

Discussion starters

Miracles

✢ What is a miracle? Do we use the term lightly?
✢ What is our view of miracles today?
✢ Do we have any examples of modern-day miracles?

Faith

✢ What does it mean to have faith in something?
✢ In what ways did Christian faith change the lives of Jesus' first disciples?
✢ In what ways does Christian faith change lives today?

Follow-up

✢ Research some people whose faith was the inspiration for their actions, such as Gladys Aylward, Florence Nightingale or Edith Cavell. What is a missionary? Do we need missionaries today?
✢ Research early Christian symbols, such as the fish and the anchor.

PSHE and Citizenship links

❖ In what ways did Jesus and his disciples operate as a team?

❖ In what ways does Andrew's eyewitness account describe friendship?

❖ What are the qualities of true friendship? (*Loyalty, trust, commitment and so on.*)

Visual demonstration

You will need: A bandage and a scarf or blindfold

Blindfold a volunteer. Ask another child to lead the blindfolded volunteer across the room. Take off the blindfold. Ask the volunteer how it felt when the blindfold was taken off.

Introduction

Jesus chose some people to be his special friends or disciples. One of them was a fisherman called Andrew. In our story, Andrew describes one of Jesus' most famous miracles. If you listen carefully, you will understand why we have a bandage to help us with the story, and also why we have experimented with a blindfold.

Eyewitness account: Andrew's story

I remember the days when Jesus taught the crowds about God. The crowds always flocked to see and hear him. His charge to tell people about God was going well. Everywhere we went, his words captured the hearts of those who listened, so that time itself seemed to stand still as they heard him speak.

On one such day, a message came to say that Mary and Martha's brother Lazarus was ill. Jesus was a close friend of that little family and we all thought that he would go straight away to help his friends, but in fact it was two more days before Jesus decided that we should go to Judea to see Lazarus.

'He is asleep,' Jesus insisted. We did not realize what he really meant until he told us clearly, 'Lazarus is dead! I'm glad I wasn't there, because now you will have a chance to put your faith in me. Let's go to him.'

What did he mean? Had we shown a lack of faith? I had always felt unworthy of being chosen to be his close friend. I'm just a simple fisherman, so how could I help in his great work? Had I disappointed him? I remembered one morning, the water of Lake Galilee clear and blue, and the sky red-orange at sunrise over distant hills. I sat with my brother Simon, looking at empty nets after a long night. Jesus told us to go out again and let down our nets for a catch. When we returned, our nets were full of writhing silver! We had seen how Jesus could change everything in an instant with his power over people on land and creatures in the sea. We had become used to amazing miracles, but had he cause to doubt our faith in him? I prayed that it was not so.

Before we entered Bethany, we found that Lazarus had already been buried. Martha rushed out to meet us. She spoke to Jesus: 'Lord, if you had been here, my brother would not have died.'

Jesus answered, 'Your brother will live again!'

Martha thought he meant that Lazarus would have life in heaven, but then Jesus said, 'I am the one who raises the dead to life! Everyone who has faith in me will live, even if they die. And everyone who lives because of faith in me will never really die. Do you believe this?'

Martha replied, 'Yes, Lord, I believe that you are Christ, the Son of God.'

Mary came out when Martha told her that Jesus had arrived. She was crying, surrounded by grieving relatives and friends.

Mary repeated Martha's words. We all knew that it was true—if Jesus had been there, Lazarus would still be alive, making us welcome in his house as he had done so often. Jesus also was overcome by emotion. He asked where Lazarus was. Mary took him to the tomb. Tears fell from the Lord's eyes and everyone knew how much he loved these friends. I heard someone behind me say, 'He gives sight to the blind. Why couldn't he have kept Lazarus from dying?'

I tried to drive the thought from my mind, even though I was plagued by the same question. We went to the tomb and Jesus, still crying, told the people to roll the stone away. Martha was there, practical as always: 'Lord, you know that Lazarus has been dead for four days, and there will be a bad smell,' she said.

Surprisingly, Jesus spoke with a touch of impatience: 'Didn't I tell you that if you had faith, you would see the glory of God?'

Standing before the open tomb, Jesus prayed, looking towards heaven: 'Father, I thank you for answering my prayer. I know that you always answer my prayers. But I said this so that people here would believe that you sent me.'

Jesus paused, then he shouted, 'Lazarus, come out!'

Everyone seemed to hold their breath. How could Jesus ask this of a man who had been dead for four days? We stood staring at the darkness of the gaping tomb. At first, all appeared still, then we sensed movement and the 'dead' man walked slowly out of the tomb, covered with strips of burial cloth. He was alive!

The onlookers gasped in amazement and then recovered themselves, rushing to help Lazarus.

Jesus said to the people, 'Untie him and let him go.'

As I say, I had witnessed many of Jesus' miracles, but now I understood what he meant when he told us to have faith in him. Nothing was impossible and yet everything had a purpose. He had waited for Lazarus to die, knowing that he would save him. Even so, the strain of knowing his dear friend had died upset him greatly.

Since the day when Jesus first chose me to be his friend, I have often marvelled at my part in his mission, but I have seen with my own eyes that, for Jesus, even death held no mystery. He could defeat it.

Follow-up questions

Why did we have a bandage to help us with this story? What did the experiment with the blindfold tell us about the story?

Suggested prayer

Dear Lord, help us to follow you as Andrew did. Help us to put our faith in you as Martha and Mary did. In this way, we may see the miracle of your love in our daily lives, leading us from darkness into light. Amen

Suggested songs

Now Jesus one day (*Someone's Singing, Lord* 30)
Shine, Jesus, shine (*Songs of Fellowship for Kids* 123)

Suggested music

'Messe Basse' from *Missa Brevis* (Fauré) (developed from the *Fishermen's Mass*)
'Mary, did you know?' from *Pure* (special edition) (Hayley Westenra)

Reflective poem: On the shores of Galilee

On the shores of Galilee
Simple fishermen,
Mending empty nets; despondent.
Jesus approaches.
In deep water, a second time:
Have faith.
Writhing, silver fish
Heaving, full nets.
Now, faith to follow,
A new catch:
People instead of fish!

A friend in need
Sleeps, in death.
Delayed footsteps
Reach a sealed tomb.
Lord, if you had been here.
Have faith!
Brother called forth,
Lazarus walks.
Bandaged body, alive!
Have faith! God's Son
Conquers death.

Christ stands
At the threshold
Between
Life and death,
Faith affirming.
Follow and believe!

Judas' story

This assembly tells the story of Palm Sunday from Judas' perspective as he realizes that Jesus does not intend to conquer the occupying Roman army by force. Disillusionment sets him on the path to betrayal.

The material may be used in the spring term to set the scene for the Easter story, or at any other time to explore ideas of PSHE and Citizenship. Judas' betrayal of Jesus is one of the key elements of the Easter story. The story is followed by a reflective poem exploring the subject of betrayal.

Bible references

Jesus enters Jerusalem

MATTHEW 21:1–11; MARK 11:1–11; LUKE 19:28–40; JOHN 12:12–19

When Jesus came to Jerusalem, everyone in the city was excited and asked, 'Who can this be?' The crowd answered, 'This is Jesus, the prophet from Nazareth in Galilee' (Matthew 21:10–11).

The Lord tells about the coming king

ZECHARIAH 9:9

Everyone in Jerusalem, celebrate and shout! Your king has won a victory, and he is coming to you. He is humble and rides on a donkey; he comes on the colt of a donkey.

Discussion starters

Betrayal

✣ Why would a friend do such a thing?

✣ If God planned for Judas to betray Jesus, should we view him in a different light? (The Church is currently considering this very question, following the publication of *The Gospel of Judas*.)

Preconceived ideas

✣ What preconceived idea did Judas have about Jesus?

✣ What preconceived ideas do we sometimes have?

✣ How does it feel to discover that we can be wrong? (*Key words: betrayal, commitment, loyalty and disappointment.*)

Terrorism

✣ The story implies that Judas found himself at odds with the peaceful approach of Jesus. He may have followed a religious, spiritual movement to achieve political ends. Consider how people who have another agenda and do not follow the spirit of the faith can use religion as a platform for political gain.

Follow-up

Judas may be hot-seated and asked questions by the class. If the other disciples had noticed how Judas felt, what might their reactions have been? Children could write an account from the point of view of one of the other disciples.

NB: This assembly links with 'Jesus' story', when Jesus speaks about the betrayal at the last supper.

Visual demonstration

> **You will need:** A palm cross, a bag with 30 silver coins inside (play money will suffice)

First of all, hold up the palm cross and ask the children if they know what it is. What is it made from? Does anyone know when and where palm crosses are given out? (*In church on Palm Sunday.*)

Ask for two volunteers. Give one volunteer the palm cross to hold and the other the bag of coins. Ask them what they have been given.

Introduction

Both of these items are important in today's story. Jesus was going into Jerusalem to celebrate the Jewish festival of Passover. His disciples were with him. This is the eyewitness story of one of them. His name was Judas. Listen carefully to see why we have a palm cross at our assembly today. Also, think about what part the bag of silver coins plays after the story has ended.

Eyewitness account: Judas' story

All the time I was with Jesus, watching the crowds flock to him, seeing their faces, their excitement, hearing them hail him as the Messiah, I had waited for one special day—the day he would ride into Jerusalem. God's Son would be taking power, returning the city to his people.

As the great day approached, I couldn't stop thinking about it. I lay awake in the night, studying the stars in the sky for signs of the great change to come, the revolution that would send Roman legionaries back to Rome, tramping hot, dusty roads towards the wrath of the emperor.

Surely the chief priests too would flee the city, or perhaps throw themselves on to the ground, prostrate in front of Jesus, hoping for mercy. I felt so proud to be one of his disciples, one of those specially selected by Jesus to help him to reclaim the promised land for the children of Israel.

It had been marvellous hearing Jesus speak about God's kingdom and actually being there when he healed people. I was becoming so used to him turning people's lives around that it almost seemed commonplace; we just expected Jesus to do these amazing things. I suppose nothing surprised us any more. In fact, to tell the truth, we would have been more surprised if he had failed to heal people.

Despite the excitement of those eventful times, I had become impatient and even irritable. Why were we waiting when there was so much to be done? Why did Jesus tolerate the Romans in the Holy City when it would be so easy for him to rid Israel of these vermin? I even asked him when we would be going to Jerusalem, but he just smiled knowingly and said, 'When the time is right in order that the prophecy may be fulfilled.'

That was all, and he would not explain any further, leaving me more bewildered and restless. What was the prophecy? Was it the end of the Roman empire and the beginning of the true glory of Israel?

As you can imagine, when the time came and we were actually on our way, I was transformed. Like an excited child, I could hardly keep still. I couldn't rest—I was so anxious to see the fulfilment of my dreams.

When we reached Bethphage at the Mount of Olives, Jesus called two of the other disciples to him and talked quietly, giving them some instructions and sending them ahead to prepare the way. He was obviously organizing a triumphant entry into Jerusalem. I didn't know how it would all happen, but my heart sang with joy and anticipation. The time had come at last! How could I have doubted for a second? Of course Jesus knew exactly how everything would be! All I had to do was wait, glowing with pride at my part in the events that would change the course of history.

As we travelled along the road, crowds seemed to grow. A feeling of anticipation surrounded us, so strongly that it almost felt as if you could touch it. It was something real, solid—the air seemed charged with a strange power. All of us sensed that a real change was coming, but Jesus remained unmoved, as calm as ever. To him, nothing was unexpected: he was like an actor playing the part that had been written for him. What that part was, I didn't know. Nor did I suspect the role I was to play in his destiny. Should I have read the signs—a look, perhaps the tone of his voice when he spoke to me? He must have known, but I did not detect even a hint of what was to come.

We approached a village not far from Jerusalem and met the disciples sent ahead by Jesus. They were leading a donkey and its colt. What could Jesus want with such lowly beasts? Where was his horse? Surely he would need a horse to ride into Jerusalem? We had to find a horse for him. I ran forward, annoyed. Was this the best they could do? They had obviously failed him.

'Where's the Master's horse?' I said impatiently. 'Can't you be trusted with anything?'

I turned to Jesus. 'Master, you should have sent me. I would have found you a great warhorse. I'm sure I still can. Please let me go?'

Jesus looked at me, his eyes suddenly filled with a strange sadness. 'They have done exactly as I asked. The words of the prophet will come true: "Your king has won a victory, and he is coming to you. He is humble and rides on a donkey."'

At that moment I knew my dreams were shattered. How could I have been so wrong? This 'king' was not riding into Jerusalem to overthrow the Romans and lead a revolution. He was going in peace, riding a donkey. A donkey! Who would have believed it?

The crowds cheered, spreading cloaks on the road and branches cut from the trees. The streets rang to the sound of praises, blessing David's son. The king had arrived in the Holy City, but it was not as I had imagined for so long.

My eyes blurred with tears. Others thought I was overcome with excitement and emotion, but the tears were tears of bitter disappointment, and the realization slowly dawned that I would bring about his downfall. I knew what I had to do.

Follow-up questions

Why did I bring a palm cross and a bag of coins? How many coins do you think there are in the bag?

Suggested prayer

Dear Lord, help us to understand that we can't always have what we want. Sometimes your purpose is not clear to us. Guide us to do what is right.

Suggested songs

Trotting, trotting (*Come and Praise 2* 128)
We have a king who rides a donkey (*Junior Praise* 264)

Suggested music

'Hosanna' from *Jesus Christ Superstar* (Rice/Lloyd Webber)

Reflective poem: Thirty pieces of silver

Thirty pieces of silver,
The cost
Of silencing the cheers,
Trampling palms strewn
For the Prince of Peace.
Dreams of war
From a friend.
Judas.

Thirty pieces of silver,
The price
Of such a life.
Jesus, Son of God,
Betrayed in the garden.
Kiss of death
From a friend.
Judas.

Thirty pieces of silver,
The reward
Lying in the dust.
Too painful to hold
In blood-stained hands.
Too late, despair
From a friend.
Judas.

Caiaphas' story

The story for this assembly takes place in the temple in Jerusalem, with the high priest having just witnessed the scene of chaos and confusion as Jesus turned over the money changers' tables. In the eyes of someone who always followed the rules, such behaviour was reprehensible!

In addition to spring term and the Easter season, this story could be used at other times to show how Jesus challenged the things he believed to be wrong. The high priest followed the rules of the Jewish law strictly and was deeply suspicious of the popularity of Jesus.

We are creatures of habit: sometimes we find new ideas difficult to accept. Even children can find the unfamiliar difficult to accept. Jesus was a dynamic individual who pushed back the barriers of a religion rooted in ancient laws and practices. People had become more involved in ritual practices than the spirituality of their faith.

The story is followed by a role-play activity to help pupils think about the attitudes taken by the different groups of people.

Bible references

Jesus in the temple

MATTHEW 21:12–17; MARK 11:15–19; LUKE 19:45–48; JOHN 2:13–22

Jesus went into the temple and chased out everyone who was selling or buying. He turned over the tables of the moneychangers and the benches of the ones who were selling doves. He told them, 'The Scriptures say, "My house should be called a place of

worship." But you have turned it into a place where robbers hide.'
... The chief priests and the teachers of the Law of Moses were
angry when they saw his miracles and heard the children shouting
praises to the Son of David (Matthew 21:12–13, 15).

Discussion starters

Faith in action

✤ What do people do to show that they follow a religion?
✤ Does it matter if someone does not follow in a particular way?
✤ What did Jesus consider to be important behaviour for those who
  believe in God?

Follow-up

Investigate people who have gone against traditions or injustice,
inspired by their faith. For example:

✤ William Wilberforce, who led the parliamentary campaign against
  the slave trade.
✤ Trevor Huddleston, who campaigned against apartheid in South
  Africa.
✤ Martin Luther King, who fought for the rights of black people in
  the USA.

Visual demonstration

You will need: Pictures of livestock, such as chickens, lambs and goats, a bag of money

The painting of *Christ Driving the Traders from the Temple* by El Greco could also be used as a visual illustration of this unit. It is available on the National Gallery website: www.nationalgallery.org.uk. Click on 'Collection' and enter El Greco in the search box.

Show the children the pictures of animals and the bag of money. Ask if they know what these things have got to do with worship at the temple in the time of Jesus. Talk about how the temple forecourts were used for buying and selling. If appropriate, show the picture by El Greco of Jesus driving the traders out of the temple.

Introduction

After riding into Jerusalem, Jesus went straight to the temple and strode into the courtyard, where the money changers traded special temple money and animals were sold for sacrifice. In our story, Caiaphas, the high priest, describes what happened when Jesus arrived.

Eyewitness account: Caiaphas' story

I remember that Passover festival so well. There was such a strange mood in the city—not the usual bustling, but a strange, serious atmosphere. I can only say it was madness. Yes, madness!

That day, the roads into the city had been lined with crowds. The people were shouting, waving palm leaves, even throwing the leaves and their own cloaks on to the ground. Now why did they do that? You may well ask! What would prompt them to do such a thing? A king, perhaps? At the very least, I hear you say. It must have been a truly great person, magnificent and powerful, to produce such a reaction.

You would be wrong! It was all for the sake of an ordinary man. A poor carpenter from Galilee—Nazareth, in fact. What was he doing? Well might you be amazed! Would you believe it? He was riding a donkey! You are no doubt thinking, perhaps he couldn't get a horse, but I was told that he asked especially for a donkey to show that he was humble and came in peace, not to make war upon the Romans.

Nevertheless, why all the fuss about a poor man on a donkey?

They called him their king, hailed him as Messiah—the anointed king, chosen by God. They said he was a descendant of our ancestor, King David, promised by the prophets long ago. Of course, I couldn't agree with that! Surely we priests at the temple would be the first to know if God had sent his anointed king. This man broke all the rules. He met with outcasts and sinners. He had even been seen healing on the sabbath. He could not be the Messiah—we had not received messages from God. I refused to believe it.

'The whole city has gone mad!' I said in bewilderment. 'Where will it end?'

Despite the commotion in Jerusalem, we continued as before, preparing our solemn celebration of the Passover festival. Life at the temple went on with the daily rituals of prayer and sacrifice. Ah well, at least here, I thought with relief, we can remain apart, stand back from the clamour and hysteria of the rest of Jerusalem. How wrong I was! My foolish pretence soon came to an end.

'He's coming!' A dusty urchin burst through the temple door from the courtyard of the money changers. I rushed to him.

'Quiet, quiet! What do you mean, interrupting our Passover celebrations? Who is coming? Whatever do you mean?'

'The teacher from Nazareth. He's right behind me. He must be here now...' He looked around excitedly, so frantic that I almost jumped in a panic.

'Ridiculous!' I managed to reply, but my thoughts rushed in every direction. Here, here in the great temple? How could this happen? I thought we would be safe here from this rule-breaker. Let him talk to the crowds on the hills and streets, not in this holy place!

I hardly knew what to do next. I raced into the courtyard as fast as my old legs would carry me. I could not believe my eyes. There was such chaos! The place was full of cries and shouts, bleating and squawking. Animals and people were charging in every direction. The money changers were shaking their fists in anger as Jesus strode around the courtyard overturning the tables, sending animals and money flying in all directions.

As he spread destruction, he shouted out, 'My house should be a place of worship, but you have turned it into a place where robbers hide.'

When Jesus had destroyed the business of the day, the watching crowds left the angry money changers to pick up the debris. I stood looking at the remains of our temple life. Sacrifice is at the heart of our rituals and it earns many a good living. What could he mean by behaviour such as this? He had brought disharmony into our ordered lives. He had set himself against our ancient practices. We have always done things in this way. I knew that I could not avoid the issue any longer. He must be stopped.

Follow-up questions

What sort of livestock was being bought and sold in the temple courtyard? Why? Why did Jesus say that the temple had been turned into a place where robbers hid? Whose 'house' was he referring to?

Suggested prayer

Dear Lord, help us to find time to talk to you quietly in prayer. Help us to see the beauty of your creation. Help us to rise above the noise and rush of our daily lives and find your peace in our hearts. Amen

Suggested songs

Lord of the dance (*Junior Praise* 91)
I will build my church (*Songs of Fellowship for Kids* 102)
It's a happy day (*Songs of Fellowship for Kids* 96)

Suggested music

'Holy City': track 15 on *Voices from Heaven* (Soweto Gospel Choir)

Role-play: At the temple

Choose eight pupils to perform the following role-play. Divide them into two groups and number the members of each group from 1 to 4. Explain that one group represents the chief priests and the other group represents the traders in the temple courtyards.

Chief priests say:

1. Jesus, the carpenter's son from Nazareth, is becoming too popular. He's breaking the rules and he's working on the sabbath.
2. Some say that he is a great prophet; he draws huge crowds wherever he goes.
3. They claim that he can cast out demons. He even said that he could forgive sins, when only God can do that.
4. He is dangerous, leading the people away from the old traditions. He is a threat to our power and the laws of the people of Israel. We must watch him carefully and wait for an opportunity to trap him.

Traders say:

1. Oh yes, I'll tell you about Jesus of Nazareth. I was at the temple, just trying to make a living, when in he rushed, shouting, and turned my table upside down.
2. I was there, too. The money flew everywhere. There were birds flapping about and animals darting in every direction. People were yelling at each other, trying to catch whatever they could before it disappeared into Jerusalem and on to someone's dinner table, no doubt!
3. Jesus said the temple was a place where robbers hide. What a cheek!
4. Well, I suppose we did make a shekel or two. It was a nice little earner! I never thought about it being wrong to use the house of God to conduct business. It seemed the obvious thing to do.

Chief priests say:

1. Yes, but now he has gone too far.
2. His downfall is assured. We will find a way to be rid of this troublesome prophet.
3. Wait a moment, who is that lurking in the shadows? Isn't that one of his friends?
4. Here's an opportunity! This angry man could be useful to us. I think we may have found a solution to the problem of how to get rid of Jesus of Nazareth.

Jesus' story

Here we meet Jesus in the intimate setting of the upper room and learn the lesson demonstrated in the simple act of foot-washing. Through the words of John's Gospel, we become eyewitnesses to Jesus' actions and hearers of his words as he prepares his disciples for his death through the symbolism of bread and wine.

This unit can be used in the spring term at the start of the Easter story. It can also be used to explain the sacrament of Holy Communion or Jesus' example of service to others (humility) and the concept of the servant-king. To help children understand what Jesus was demonstrating by washing the feet of his disciples, the story is followed by a practical re-enactment of the foot-washing scene.

It may be necessary to explain the significance of Holy Communion (also known as the Eucharist, the Lord's Supper or, in the Catholic tradition, Mass). A member of the clergy could come into school to help pupils to learn about the importance of the service of Holy Communion to Christians.

NB: The assembly continues to explore the theme of betrayal, first introduced in Judas' story (see page 21).

Bible references

Jesus washes the feet of his disciples

JOHN 13:1–30

During the meal Jesus got up, removed his outer garment, and wrapped a towel around his waist. He put some water into a large bowl. Then he began washing his disciples' feet and drying them with the towel he was wearing (vv. 4–5).

The Lord's Supper

MARK 14:22–24

During the meal Jesus took some bread in his hands. He blessed the bread and broke it. Then he gave it to his disciples and said, 'Take this. It is my body.' Jesus picked up a cup of wine and gave thanks to God. He gave it to his disciples, and said, 'Drink it!' So they all drank some. Then he said, 'This is my blood, which is poured out for many people, and with it God makes his agreement.'

Discussion starters

Citizenship

The story demonstrates the importance of service to others and the way in which Jesus instructed his disciples to follow this vocation.

✢ How can we be of service to others?
✢ Does helping others always need to be an act of humility?
✢ What examples do we have of people devoting their lives to the service of others because of their Christian faith?

Follow-up

Research the lives of people who have devoted their lives to the service of others because of Christianity, such as Mother Teresa and Florence Nightingale. Also research people such as Father Kolbe, who made the ultimate sacrifice of giving their lives for the sake of others.

Visual demonstration

> **You will need:** A large bowl, a jug of water, a towel, a picture of the Jesus washing the disciples' feet

For the picture, you could use one from *The Life of Jesus through the Eyes of an Artist*, or the *Last Supper* by Leonardo da Vinci, or *The Sacrament of the Last Supper* by Salvador Dali (see page 125 for details).

Choose two pupils to help you with a foot-washing re-enactment. Ask one pupil to wash the feet of the other and dry them with a towel.

Introduction

Explain to the children that the re-enactment they have just seen demonstrates what Jesus did for his disciples during the meal they shared together just before the end of Jesus' life. The meal has come to be known as the last supper.

Eyewitness account: Jesus' story

I knew the time had come to return to my heavenly Father, and that I would undergo terrible cruelty and pain before my task in this world was completed. As the time of Passover drew near, I planned a final meal with my disciples as part of the festival celebrations—a farewell before the horror began.

The small room was peaceful in the candlelight. Outside,

a multitude of stars lit up the sky. As well as pain, this earthly life contains such beauty and wonder, a soul-soothing warmth for the spirit.

As we gathered together, my friends and I, the atmosphere was sombre and subdued. We are not always as solemn as some may think. Our work is joyful, and the mood is often light, with happy exchanges among the group. That night, however, the air hung heavy with expectation. They did not know my purpose in Jerusalem, but I think they sensed my apprehension.

During the meal, I arose from the table and prepared to wash the dust of the streets from their feet. Laying aside my outer robe, I wrapped a towel around my waist like an apron. Simon Peter questioned my actions. He seemed so indignant that I was taking the role normally given to a servant. I explained that I needed to set them an example of servanthood: I needed to wash the feet of each person in that room. Apart from the dust on their feet, they were all 'clean', except one. The traitor smiled and thanked me as the others did. I met his eyes and tried to look into his soul, but saw only darkness. Satan had taken possession of the man I had known as Judas, yet I knew his betrayal would fulfil the ancient prophecy. He had his part to play.

After I had washed their feet, again I took my place at the table. I wanted them to understand what I had done for them. I wanted them to serve each other as I had served them. I also needed them to know what would happen to me. I took some bread in my hands. I lifted it in thanks to God my Father and broke it into pieces. Offering each of my friends a piece of the bread, I told them, 'Take this. It is my body.' I then took a cup of wine and, again, lifted it in thanks to my heavenly Father. 'Drink this,' I said. 'It is my blood.'

Strange words, strange actions, but I needed them to know that, through the breaking of my body and the spilling of my blood, my Father's agreement would be sealed and the doors of heaven opened to all who believed. I asked them to do this when they were gathered together, to remember me.

I was deeply troubled by all that lay ahead. Knowing what must be done, I hastened the deed. 'I tell you for certain that one of you will betray me,' I told them. They were dumb-struck, unbelieving. Peter asked, 'Lord, which one of us are you talking about?' I dipped the bread into a bowl of olive oil and gave it to Judas, the son of Simon Iscariot. Satan indeed filled his heart and soul. I had no doubt that he would complete his task.

'Judas, go quickly and do what you have to do.'

He took the bread from my hand. He would not lift his eyes to mine. Quickly and silently, he rose from the table and went out into the night. As the door closed behind him, I glanced again out of the window. It seemed to me that the light of the stars had dimmed. Evil wants to hide its face, I thought sadly. It had begun!

Follow-up questions

Why would it have been usual to wash visitors' feet? (*It was the custom to wash the dust from a visitor's feet as a sign of welcome.*) Who would have done this? (*A servant.*) What do you think Jesus was demonstrating when he washed the feet of his disciples? (*That we should serve each other with humility.*)

Suggested prayer

Help us to serve others, Lord, as Jesus did, by following his example. May we never count ourselves too important to be of service to others. In the name of your Son, Jesus Christ. Amen

Suggested songs

The servant king (*Songs of Fellowship for Kids* 31)
Give me oil in my lamp (*Come and Praise 1* 43)
Jesus' hands were kind hands (*Junior Praise* 134)

Suggested music

Dominus Jesus in Qua Nocte (Palestrina)
'The Last Supper' from *Jesus Christ Superstar* (Rice/Lloyd Webber)

Reflective poem: The Last Supper

Here, friends gathered,
Meal of fellowship,
Journey of memories,
Some spoken, some held silent,
Voices, smiles, laughter.

Here, friends contented,
Warm fellowship,
Passover celebration.
Do they know
What lies ahead?

Here, friends solemn,
Symbols of fellowship,
My body, my blood
Given for you.

Here, friends thoughtful,
Broken fellowship,
Oil of bread and lamp.
My eyes search the dark soul
Of the betrayer.

Marcus' story

The backdrop to this assembly is the garden of Gethsemane. In the middle of the night, in darkness and confusion, a Roman soldier is following orders. (We have called him Marcus.) Somehow, he senses that this is no ordinary arrest and the man they are arresting is no ordinary person. His disquiet at the events leads to reflective thoughts.

The Roman occupation of first-century Palestine is the historical context of this story. Pupils should be made aware that the Roman army were an occupying force at the time of Jesus. They may have studied Roman Britain and have an understanding of the structure of the Roman army. This knowledge helps to emphasize the place of Jesus in history. Palestine is the name commonly used for the land bordering the Mediterranean Sea to the west, the River Jordan to the east, the Lebanon range to the north and the Sinai desert to the south, in ancient times. Gethsemane was the name of the garden on the slopes of the Mount of Olives just outside Jerusalem.

The story is followed by a reflective poem, showing that Gethsemane has come to mean more than just the name of the garden where the events took place.

Bible references

Jesus prays

MATTHEW 26:36–46; MARK 14:32–42; LUKE 22:39–46

Jesus went with his disciples to a place called Gethsemane, and he told them, 'Sit here while I pray' (Mark 14:32).

Jesus is arrested

MATTHEW 26:47–56; MARK 14:43–50; LUKE 22:47–53; JOHN 18:3–12

Judas had promised to betray Jesus. So he went to the garden with some Roman soldiers and temple police, who had been sent by the chief priests and the Pharisees. They carried torches, lanterns, and weapons. Jesus already knew everything that was going to happen, but he asked, 'Who are you looking for?' They answered, 'We are looking for Jesus from Nazareth!' (John 18:3–5).

Discussion starters

Gethsemane

❖ The garden of Gethsemane was a quiet, peaceful place. What places do you know where you can find peace and quiet?

❖ There are two main characters and two main groups of people in our story today: Jesus and his disciples, Judas and the Roman soldiers. The thoughts and feelings of the different characters and groups would have been very varied. What do you think they might have been?

Follow-up

This story lends itself very well to a drama presentation or a freeze-frame re-enactment. Set the scene in the garden. Jesus is praying. The disciples fall asleep a little way off. The soldiers approach with Judas, who is showing his nerves at the terrible act he is about to perform. Jesus knew what was going to happen to him, yet he prayed that he would not have to go through it. Finally, he accepted God's will with calm composure.

Use the questions above to set the scene and re-enact the drama. Use a freeze-frame to explore the feelings of the people present as the events unfold.

Choose pupils to hot-seat:

✣ A soldier who had to carry out the arrest
✣ A disciple: had he failed Jesus by falling asleep?
✣ Jesus: how did he feel, knowing all that lay ahead?

Pupils could write poems or their own accounts of the events in the garden of Gethsemane.

PSHE and Citizenship links

Explore the subject of courage. Jesus showed courage in the face of the terrible cruelty he was about to endure. Christians believe that Jesus can help us to face the challenges of our daily lives.

Visual demonstration

You will need: A lantern, a toy sword, toy armour, a picture of Roman soldiers, a picture of Jesus being arrested.

For the picture of Jesus' arrest, use the example from *The Life of Jesus through the Eyes of an Artist* (see page 125 for details).

Place the lantern on a table so that everyone can see it. Show the sword and armour. Ask the children who would wear these items. Show the picture of Roman soldiers. Ask the children if anyone knows which army they are from.

Introduction

Explain that the Roman army was the occupying force at the time of Jesus. Today's story is written from the point of view of one of the Roman soldiers. His name is Marcus. After sharing a last meal (the meal that we now know as the last supper) with his disciples, Jesus went to the garden of Gethsemane to pray. He asked his friends to keep watch a short distance away, but they fell asleep.

As they listen to the story, ask the children to think about why the story needs a lantern. Tell them to listen for the person in the story who has a lantern and see if they know who he is.

Eyewitness account: Marcus' story

It was a gloomy morning before cockcrow when we left the guardroom on orders to make an arrest.

'Oh well, I'm tired of cleaning. This armour must be the

brightest in the legion by now!' laughed Maximus. 'Anyway,' he added, 'this should be an easy one.'

'Who are we arresting?' I asked, placing my sword in its scabbard.

Maximus reached for his shield and replied, 'Only a religious teacher—a man from Galilee. You may have heard of him. He comes from the town of Nazareth.'

'Why are they sending ten of us to arrest a man of God? Will he fight? Surely three or four would be enough.' I moaned, knowing that my armour would not pass the attention of the centurion. I needed more cleaning time!

'He has friends and he's popular. Were you there the other day when he rode into the city?'

I remembered the commotion.

'I heard about it,' I replied. 'They said he was on a donkey, but the people were calling him the Messiah, God's chosen one. There was trouble afterwards at the temple.'

'Well,' grinned Maximus, 'we'll see if there's trouble today!'

We joined the others and were led across the city to Gethsemane, a garden on a hillside. The air was still but the gloomy feeling I had felt earlier would not lift, despite Maximus' assurances of an easy arrest. I'll be glad to see the sunrise, I thought.

Waiting in the dark, by the gate, stood a figure with a lantern. The light distorted his swarthy face. He beckoned to us with a sly, conspiratorial glance back over his shoulder as if he expected to have been followed. So, the Nazarene was popular—perhaps too popular, if a friend betrayed him. Why? Jealousy? Money? I shrugged my shoulders. It was usually money! But a friend? Surely he knew what was likely to happen? We made our way through the garden as the sky reddened with the coming of the new day. The air felt chilled… or was that my imagination?

We approached a group of huddled figures. Our pace quickened but we still moved silently. They appeared to rouse themselves from a dreamlike state, unaware of their surroundings or of the looming danger. Further away, a lone figure knelt, head bowed in prayer. He could not have heard us but he rose and turned slowly, meeting our eyes with a steady gaze. He stepped forward as if to greet a friend. I saw him search for the familiar face among the soldiers, showing no surprise, just resignation, acceptance. His betrayer tried to look into the deep eyes, flickered fear, turned to leave, then seemed to reconsider and stepped forward, greeting the teacher with an embrace.

We did not need the signal to know that this was the man. He was obviously expecting us, as though we were part of his plan. Maximus is right, I thought, this man won't fight. We grabbed hold of Jesus and arrested him—it was as easy as taking a baby lamb. Just as I thought it was over, one of his followers sprang up with an angry cry and rushed forward, brandishing a sword. He lashed out, striking off the ear of Malchus, the servant of the high priest, who howled with pain.

'Enough of that!' The cry came from the man we'd come to arrest. His followers fell back, reluctant, realizing that it was hopeless. He meant to be taken.

What happened next, I hardly dare to write. This man— the one we had come to arrest—healed Malchus' severed ear!

With calm hands, he reached out and restored Malchus to health, as if nothing had happened. Am I, too, guilty just by my very words as I report this? I fear that my superiors would say I am, but I cannot help but wonder… Who is this man who is now in our charge?

Follow-up questions

Ask the children why the story needs a lantern. Who has the lantern? Who has the sword?

Suggested prayer

Father God, grant us the serenity to accept the things we cannot change, the courage to change the things we can, and the wisdom to know the difference. Amen

REINHOLD NIEBUHR (1892–1971)

Suggested songs

Jesus in the garden (*Come and Praise 2* 129)
Father, hear the prayer we offer (*Junior Praise* 41)

Suggested music

'Behold, my saviour now is taken' from *St Matthew Passion* (J.S. Bach)
'And they came to a place named Gethsemane' and 'The agony' from *The Crucifixion* (John Stainer)
'Gethsemane (I only want to say)' from *Jesus Christ Superstar* (Rice/Lloyd Webber)

Reflective poem: Gethsemane

Under the gnarled old tree
in the garden,
Who comes?
A quiet man who prays,
His sweat dripping into bare stones.
Friends sleep at a distance.
Do they know his anguish?

Under the gnarled old tree
in the garden,
Who comes?
A friend, with a kiss of greeting.
What is this mocking embrace?
Surprise? No! Expected.
Who recognizes the betrayer?

Under the gnarled old tree
in the garden,
Who comes?
Servants of the chief priests
Seeking their prey,
Destroying God's Son
Through ignorance and fear.
Can they hide their shame?

Under the gnarled old tree
in the garden,
Who comes?
Roman soldiers, swords glinting,
Following orders.
A night's work quickly done.
Why do we arrest a man of
God?

Under the gnarled old tree in
the garden,
Who comes?
A friend who fights,
Roused suddenly,
An ear severed, quickly healed.
Who has the power to heal?

Under the gnarled old tree in
the garden,
Who comes?
Only silent shades
Drifting in the mist.
Echoes of the night's events.
Could there have been another
way?

Under the gnarled old tree in
the garden,
In the dark of the night
It begins.

Peter's story (1)

After his arrest, Jesus is led away to the house of Caiaphas, the high priest. Peter has followed at a distance. In the courtyard, disturbing events unfold, which lead to Peter denying ever having known Jesus. As the sun starts to rise, a cockerel crows and Peter breaks down in tears as he realizes that Jesus' words have come true.

As well as during the Easter season, the material could be used at any time to consider the life of Jesus' disciple Peter, and to demonstrate friendship and loyalty. This assembly links to the story of Peter in Unit 12 (see pages 93–100) and the stories of the ascension and Pentecost in Units 13 and 14 (see pages 101–114).

Bible references

Peter's promise

MATTHEW 26: 31–35; MARK 14:27–31; LUKE 22:31–34; JOHN 13:36–38

Simon Peter asked, 'Lord, where are you going?' Jesus answered, 'You can't go with me now, but later on you will.' Peter asked, 'Lord, why can't I go with you now? I would die for you!' 'Would you really die for me?' Jesus asked. 'I tell you for certain that before a cock crows, you will say three times that you don't even know me' (John 13:36–38).

Peter says he doesn't know Jesus

MATTHEW 26:69–75; MARK 14:66–72; LUKE 22:56–62; JOHN18:15–18, 25–27

While Peter was still in the courtyard, a servant girl of the high priest came up and saw Peter warming himself by the fire. She stared at him and said, 'You were with Jesus from Nazareth!' Peter replied, 'That isn't true! I don't know what you're talking about. I don't have any idea what you mean' (Mark 14:66–68).

Discussion starters

Denial

✢ How might the servant girl have recognized Peter?

✢ Have you ever made a promise that you later could not keep? How did you feel?

✢ Why did Peter break down in tears when he heard the cockerel crow?

Follow-up

People in Jerusalem could tell that Peter was from Galilee because of his accent. Discuss regional accents. Do we judge people by their accents? Why? Choose a pupil to hot-seat Peter and ask the children to question him about his experience in the courtyard of the high priest's house.

PSHE and Citizenship links

Discuss friendship and loyalty and link this to courage and forgiveness (see Unit 12 for the story of Jesus forgiving Peter). Research the life of Peter and the early Church. After Jesus had forgiven him, Peter demonstrated his loyalty to Jesus and became the rock on which the Christian Church was founded.

Visual demonstration

You will need: A picture of a cockerel, or the sound of a cockerel crowing

Show the children the picture of the cockerel, or play the sound of a cockerel crowing. Ask the children if they have ever heard a cockerel crowing. At what time of day might we hear a cockerel crowing?

Introduction

Explain that after Jesus was arrested, he was taken to the house of Caiaphas, the high priest. Jesus' close friend, Peter, followed at a distance to see if he could find out what was happening. He stood in the courtyard of the high priest's house, warming his hands by the fire. In the story, the children need to listen for the sound of the cockerel crowing and think about why it was important.

Eyewitness account: Peter's story

'You fools! Why didn't you try to stop them?'

I ran to the others, the sword with which I had lashed out at the high priest's servant still in my trembling hand.

'But the master…' James started to say, his eyes wide with disbelief.

I looked at his tear-streaked face and suddenly I remembered. A cold thought crept into my mind like a thief in the night. Judas!

'Where is he?' I turned quickly and ran into the shadows,

frantic and angry. 'Where is he? The traitor! The betrayer!'

Why did I think he would still be there, still watching? Did I think he would be standing in the shadows with a look of smug satisfaction on his gaunt face, enjoying the results of his night's work? Reality dawned in my stunned mind and I knew I was wrong. He would not stay a moment longer than he had to. Judas! What a coward! He was no better than a rat crawling back to its sewer. He was beneath contempt. There was no point in pursuing him.

No, I would not search for Judas, but I knew I had to do something. Sleep would not come this dreadful night. I turned again to the others.

'I'm going after him!' I cried out. 'I must find out where they are taking him.' In the darkness, I could hear the sound of the soldiers' footsteps. I began my pursuit, following at a distance, out of sight, not wishing to put myself in danger of being spotted.

Eventually, I arrived at the house of Caiaphas, the high priest. The servants had built a fire in the courtyard. I was drawn towards it, the cold shock that gripped my heart worse than the chill air of the dying night. People sat round the fire; news of the arrest of Jesus was on everyone's lips. I sat quietly, almost in a dreamlike state, watching images of his face amid the flames. He had appeared so calm at the traitor's greeting—accepting the embrace of a friend turned enemy.

My thoughts and the vivid pictures of the events that had shattered the gentle peace of that quiet garden drifted with the smoke into the cold air. I tried to tell myself that it was not real, that it didn't happen. But grim reality kicked against my numbed senses.

At first I didn't see the servant girl, or, if I did, I was not aware of her. Her words shook me out of the stupor of my thoughts.

'This man was with Jesus!' She stared at me as she spoke the words of condemnation.

'Woman, I don't even know that man!'

I lied like a coward, desperately trying to save my own skin. I shook with fear. Why had I come here? It was too dangerous. Suddenly, I was afraid to move quickly, to be seen to panic. I had to stay where I was and give the appearance of normality. I mustn't show my anxiety. I stretched my hands towards the warmth of the fire and tried to seem unhurried. Whispers grew around me. She had planted a seed in their minds.

'You are one of them!' A voice echoed her thoughts.

'No, I'm not!' I said with as much conviction as I could.

Why didn't I leave while I had the chance? The truth is, I just sat there, wrapped in my cloak as if to hide my fear and shame. I don't know how much time passed, but my terror went on.

'This man *must* have been with Jesus. They both came from Galilee.'

I rose in feigned anger.

'I don't know what you are talking about!' I shouted.

My words were silenced by the crowing of a cockerel. I spun round and looked up, and there, in the fire's light, I saw him. Jesus was standing on the balcony above the courtyard. At the sound of the cockerel, he turned and looked at me. I caught my Lord's eye across the darkness of the courtyard. His look pierced my very soul. In the silence that followed,

I remembered his words: 'Before a cock crows tomorrow morning, you will say three times that you don't know me.'

I fled from the courtyard in a blind panic. Bitter tears of self-loathing consumed me. I had proved him right. I had failed him.

Follow-up questions

Why did Peter say he didn't know Jesus? Why was the crowing of the cockerel important?

Suggested prayer

Dear Lord, help us to be there when we are needed. Help us to know when to lend a helping hand or listening ear. Give us the courage to say sorry if we have done something wrong, and the strength to forgive others for the wrong they do to us. Amen

Suggested songs

Great is your faithfulness (*Junior Praise* 64)
When I needed a neighbour (*Junior Praise* 275)
What a friend we have in Jesus (*Junior Praise* 273)

Suggested music

'O man, bemoan thy grievous sin' from *St Matthew Passion* (J.S. Bach)
'Thy rebuke hath broken his heart' and 'Behold, and see if there be any sorrow' from *Messiah* (G.F. Handel)

Reflective drama: Do you know him?

Rehearse this simple drama before the assembly so that the children can deliver their lines with confidence.

You will need:
- ✛ Five children to play narrators (1–5)
- ✛ Six children to play the high priest's servants (1–6)
- ✛ A centurion
- ✛ A disciple
- ✛ Peter
- ✛ Jesus
- ✛ Up to four Roman soldiers

Narrator 1: When Jesus was arrested in the garden, the soldiers took him to the house of Caiaphas, the high priest.

Centurion: Quick march! Prisoner's guard, halt!

Soldiers, Jesus and one disciple go into the courtyard of the high priest's house.

Disciple: Where are you taking him?

Soldier: To the high priest. You can come into the courtyard.

Peter appears but stays by the gate.

Narrator 2: The other disciple spoke to the servant at the gate and she let Peter go in.

Servant 1: Aren't you one of the disciples of Jesus of Galilee?

Peter: I don't know what you are talking about.

Narrator 3: The servants and guards had lit a fire and were standing round it. It was cold, so they were warming themselves by the fire.

Servant 1: *(To Peter)* It's a cold night. Come and warm yourself by the fire.

Peter goes to stand with them, murmuring his thanks.

Servant 2: Yes. We are all in need of warmth. There's a chill in the air—I fear that cold deeds have taken place this night.

Servant 3: They've arrested the good teacher from Nazareth and they're looking for his followers.

Servant 4: *(Pointing to Peter)* He was with Jesus of Nazareth.

Servant 5: Yes, didn't I see you with him in the garden?

Peter: I swear that I don't know that man!

Servant 6: Of course you are one of them. The way you speak gives you away.

Peter: I am telling the truth. May God punish me if I am not! I do not know him!

Narrator 4: Three times they asked him and three times he denied knowing Jesus. As Peter answered them for the third time, he heard the distant crowing of a cockerel.

Narrator 5: It was just as Jesus had said.

Jesus turns and looks at Peter; everyone else freezes.

Jesus: I tell you for certain that before a cock crows, you will say three times that you don't even know me.

Peter falls to his knees, his head in his hands, weeping.

Reflective poem: The watcher

Who watches
In the shadows?

As fire flames flicker,
Footsteps on courtyard cobbles;
Cautious creeping,

Keeping a safe distance.

Do you know him?

You are one of them.
You were with him.
You are from Galilee.

No! No! No!

Three times
In the misty morning
A cock crows.

Prophetic sign,
A friend in fear
Turns away.

Pilate's story

In the Roman government of first-century Palestine, the regions of Judea and Samaria were governed by procurators sent out from Rome. Pontius Pilate was the governor of Judea and Samaria from AD26 to 37. The Jewish Council (the Sanhedrin) condemned Jesus to death for blasphemy, but it had no power to carry out the death sentence. Only the Roman governor could authorize execution. The religious authorities therefore needed to convince Pilate that Jesus was a traitor to Rome and ought to be executed. Pilate is chiefly remembered for the part he played in the trial and crucifixion of Jesus.

This assembly can be used in the spring term as a preparation for Easter. Equally, it can be used as part of a project on the life of Jesus.

Bible references

Pontius Pilate

LUKE 3:1

For fifteen years Emperor Tiberius had ruled that part of the world. Pontius Pilate was governor of Judea, and Herod was the ruler of Galilee.

Jesus is tried by Pilate

MATTHEW 27:11–26; MARK 15:1–15; LUKE 23:1–5, 15–25; JOHN 18:28–40; 19:1–16

'You know I'm not a Jew!' Pilate said. 'Your own people and the chief priests brought you to me. What have you done?' Jesus answered, 'My kingdom doesn't belong to this world. If it did, my followers would have fought to keep me from being handed over to the Jewish leaders. No, my kingdom doesn't belong to this world' (John 18:35–36).

The death sentence

MATTHEW 27:24

Pilate saw that there was nothing he could do and that the people were starting to riot. So he took some water and washed his hands in front of them and said, 'I won't have anything to do with killing this man. You are the ones doing it!'

Discussion starters

Cowardice

✣ Pilate's decision has been seen as an act of cowardice. Do you agree?

Follow-up

After pupils have heard the story, hold a debate to discuss Pilate's actions: 'This house believes that Pontius Pilate was a coward who should have exercised his power to stop the execution of Jesus.'

PSHE and Citizenship links

Explore the following topics with pupils. In what ways might a belief in God help with these actions?

✣ Making decisions
✣ Standing up for what is right even if it is unpopular
✣ Using responsibility wisely

Visual demonstration

You will need: A bowl of water and a towel, a picture of Pilate questioning Jesus

For the picture, use 'Pilate questions Jesus' from *The Life of Jesus through the Eyes of an Artist*, or *Ecce Homo* by Antonio Ciseri, or *Christ before Pilate* by Tintoretto (see page 125 for details).

Make a show of washing your hands in the bowl of water and drying them with the towel. Ask the question, 'What does it mean when we say "I wash my hands of it"?'

Introduction

After Jesus was arrested, he was taken before the high priest, Caiaphas, who was the leader of the Jewish Council. Caiaphas wanted to get rid of Jesus because he saw him as a troublemaker. The charge against Jesus was blasphemy.

Caiaphas sent Jesus to Pontius Pilate, who was the Roman governor. Pilate was a powerful man but he found himself in a difficult position because, although he didn't find Jesus guilty of any crime, he did not want to cause the Jewish community to riot. It was for this reason that Pilate 'washed his hands' of the matter and allowed Jesus to be condemned to death.

Eyewitness account: Pilate's story

I am a powerful man and, I like to think, a firm ruler of the Jewish people in this land occupied by the might of Rome. Here, I *am* Rome. I make the decisions, choosing life or death.

There are few nights when I do not sleep easy in my bed, satisfied that Roman justice has prevailed over the different tribes and religious groups that go to make up the region of Judea. Despite my confidence, however, this Passover my nights have been disturbed and I have lain awake, my tormented mind filled with accusation.

The problem is that the Jewish chief priests arrested a man and sent him to me. His name was Jesus and he was accused of blasphemy against their God. He seems to have claimed that he was God's chosen Messiah. So I asked him directly, 'Are you the king of the Jews?' But he only answered, 'Those are your words!' He then clammed up on me and would say nothing further.

How could I condemn a man on such a charge? He had done nothing wrong in the eyes of Rome and he appeared calm and reasonable—almost serene, considering what he was going through. He stood passively, waiting for judgment. He didn't whine and plead as many have done, shaking with fear before me. Should I send this man to his death? After all, it was not *my* religion he was accused of blaspheming. Why should I be drawn into the power struggles of the Jewish chief priests? They are a thorn in my side anyway—sanctimonious charlatans, in my view. What had he done to deserve such a fate?

Now the thing is that, during Passover, it is the custom for me to free a prisoner chosen by the people. This might have been the resolution I was seeking! This year, a well-known terrorist named Jesus Barabbas was in jail. Surely the people would ask me to release the innocent prisoner and condemn the guilty. I went outside to the crowd, who were gathered at my gates.

'Which prisoner do you want me to set free?' I asked them.

'Barabbas!' they replied.

Barabbas! I could not believe that they wanted me to free a terrorist instead of this peaceful, good man who had not committed a crime. But I could not afford to displease the emperor of Rome by allowing a riot in Jerusalem, so I had to set Barabbas free. I gave orders for Jesus to be beaten. My soldiers dressed him in a crown of thorns and a purple robe—a mock king for the crowd to jeer at. Perhaps, I thought, that would satisfy them.

But still the crowd bayed for his blood—egged on by the chief priests, I'll be bound.

'Nail him to a cross!' they yelled out.

I had looked into the eyes of the prisoner before me. He was no mad man with wild claims. I felt a sickness rise in my stomach. I spoke to him again. 'Where are you from?'

He would not answer me. Did he want to die? I asked myself this question over and over again, and I have not stopped asking it since. I wanted to set him free—I had the power to do so. Why should I do the bidding of the rabble in the streets? I am Pilate, the governor of Judea. Surely I should show my strength. Surely I should not be their puppet.

But then, they cried out, 'If you set this man free, you are no friend of the emperor. Anyone who claims to be king is an enemy of the emperor.'

Again I tried to reason with them. 'Look at your king,' I implored them as I showed him to the crowd.

'Kill him! Kill him!' they roared. 'Nail him to a cross!'

'So you want me to nail your king to a cross?' I asked them. The cunning chief priests replied, 'The emperor is our king!' and I knew they had won. I washed my hands of the decision. In front of the people, I showed them that I didn't want to have anything to do with the killing of this innocent man. Then I set Barabbas free and handed Jesus over to be nailed to a cross.

Follow-up questions

Pilate didn't find Jesus guilty. Why didn't he let him go?

Suggested prayer

Dear Lord, give us strength to do what is right, even when it is difficult. Be with us when we are tempted to take the easy way. Help us to see the truth and to hear your guiding voice. Amen

Suggested songs

You laid aside your majesty (*Songs of Fellowship for Kids* 195)
What kind of love is this? (*Songs of Fellowship for Kids* 184)
Jesus in the garden (*Come and Praise 2* 129)

Suggested music

'Trial by Pilate' from *Jesus Christ Superstar* (Rice/Lloyd Webber)
'How falsely doth the world accuse' and 'To witness false my Saviour answ'reth not' from *St Matthew Passion* (J.S. Bach)
Go forth into the world in peace (John Rutter)

Reflective news report: The Daily Israelite

The news report below can be read as a presentation piece in assembly. Pupils could also write their own reports dealing with this or any other event of the Easter story.

THE DAILY ISRAELITE

AD33 10 SHEKELS

'KING' TO BE CRUCIFIED!

The religious teacher Jesus of Nazareth is to be crucified today (Friday) for claiming to be the king of the Jews. Jesus has caused nothing but trouble over the past three years, healing people on the sabbath and generally giving religious leaders a hard time. Earlier this week, he caused a commotion when he rode into the city on a donkey. The crowd seemed to love it! They were shouting 'Hosanna!' and laying palm leaves on the road in front of him, as if it were the most natural thing in the world. Later on, Jesus overturned the money changers' tables in the temple, upsetting more than just their wares. 'He has defied the laws of Israel,' insisted Caiaphas, the chief priest.

Jesus was taken into custody on Thursday. His arrest was aided and abetted by one of his own followers, Judas Iscariot. After Caiaphas had questioned Jesus, he was sent to be tried by our Roman governor, Pontius Pilate. According to the tradition at Passover, allowing people to choose a prisoner to be set free, Pilate offered to release either Jesus or the renowned terrorist, Barabbas. Although Pilate declared Jesus innocent of any crime, the people insisted that Barabbas should be freed and Jesus condemned to death. Pilate said, 'I won't have anything to do with the killing of this man.' As he said this, he washed his hands in front of the crowd.

VISIT JACOB'S MARKET STALL
for olives, figs, lemons and other fine fruits. Highest standards.
Daily deliveries.

Good Friday's story

This assembly endeavours to capture the sense of defeat and despair that Jesus' followers felt on the day we know as Good Friday. When Jesus died on the cross, his followers thought that everything was over. Their minds were closed by grief to the promise of eternity that Jesus had taught through his words and demonstrated through his actions.

This assembly can be used in the week before the end of the spring term or in the week before Easter. Equally, it can be used as part of a project on the life of Jesus.

The process of crucifixion should be explained, including the practice of breaking the legs of those being crucified to hasten death by causing the lungs to collapse. As described in John 19:31–33, Jesus did not have his legs broken, because he was already dead. This fulfilled the prophecy, 'No bone of his body will be broken' (John 19:36; see Psalm 34:20).

Bible references

The death of Jesus

MATTHEW 27:32–56; MARK 15:21–41; LUKE 23:26–49; JOHN 19:16–37

Jesus said, 'Father, forgive these people! They don't know what they're doing' (Luke 23:34).

The officer and the soldiers guarding Jesus felt the earthquake and saw everything else that happened. They were frightened and said, 'This man really was God's Son!' (Matthew 27:54).

Discussion starters

Forgiveness

Jesus forgave those who put him to death (Luke 23:34). Christians try to follow Jesus' great example of forgiveness.

❖ Think of a time when you needed to be forgiven. How did it feel to need forgiveness? How did it feel to receive forgiveness?
❖ How does it feel to forgive someone when they have wronged you?

Follow-up

Pupils could write poems about the events of Good Friday. They could then compare the death of Jesus to the joy of the resurrection (see Unit 9 on pages 71–77). Pupils could also hot-seat the Roman centurion who was guarding Jesus. Remind them that hot cross buns are traditionally eaten on Good Friday to remind Christians of Jesus' death on the cross.

PSHE and Citizenship links

The story of Good Friday could provide an opportunity to talk about death and feelings of loss and grief. It is important to say that death is a natural process that happens to everyone. Christians believe that, through Jesus' death and resurrection, God promises eternal life to all who believe in him.

Visual demonstration

You will need: A simple wooden cross, a hot cross bun, a picture of the crucifixion.

For the picture, you could use 'Jesus is nailed to a cross' from *The Life of Jesus through the Eyes of an Artist*, or *Yellow Crucifixion* by Marc Chagall (1943) (see page 125 for details).

Show the children the wooden cross. Do they know why the cross is a symbol of Christianity? On which day do Christians remember Jesus' death? *(Good Friday.)* Why is this day called Good Friday? *(It is a corruption of 'God's Friday'—the day when God died for the sins of the world.)* Remind the children that hot cross buns are traditionally eaten by Christians on Good Friday in remembrance of Jesus' death on the cross.

Eyewitness account: the death of Jesus

The poem below is designed to be used in place of an eyewitness account. It may be used as part of an assembly or in church as part of an Easter service for the school. The poem can be read by a member of staff or clergy, or it can be rehearsed and presented by a pupil.

Follow-up questions

The intention is that the poem should be followed by a short silence, so there are no follow-up questions.

Death

Death waits.
A silent, patient presence.
Smiling, pale and gaunt.
Pain, a road
Leading to the icy embrace
Of the cold tomb.

Dark, the Grim Reaper,
Scythe raised,
Surveys the scene.
Three crosses,
Golgotha:
The place of the skull.
Home territory.

The scent of decay
Hangs in the air.
How dismal,
The blackest day,
Turned to night.
Evil deeds stain
Creation.

Violence, blood, despair,
All hope banished.
Forlorn onlookers weep
While cruel tormentors
Sink hell's gates.
No mercy.

It is done.
Death strides swiftly
To gather his prey.
Sombre satisfaction.
The great prize
Broken, defeated.

Is this the end?
Has God's Son
Paid the price
For our wrongdoing?
The light of hope flickers,
Death's deadly smile fades.
Who has won this battle?

Suggested prayer

Dear Lord, thank you for sending your Son, Jesus Christ, to die for us and to show us how to live. Amen

Suggested songs

There is a green hill, far away (*Junior Praise* 245)
When I survey the wondrous cross (*Junior Praise* 277)

Suggested music

'Crucifixion' from *Jesus Christ, Superstar* (Rice/Lloyd Webber)
'Jesus said, "Father, forgive them!"' from *The Crucifixion* (John Stainer)
'Agnus Dei' from *The Armed Man* (Karl Jenkins)

Mary Magdalene's story

Mary describes her feelings about the death of Jesus. She is going to the tomb to anoint the body with oils and spices, with some of the other women. After finding the tomb empty, Mary tells the disciples but goes back to the tomb, overcome with grief. It is then that she encounters the risen Christ.

When Mary told the disciples that she had seen Jesus, they did not believe her. It is significant that she was the first person to see Jesus, as women were regarded as unreliable witnesses. The assembly story is drawn from the accounts in both Mark's Gospel and John's Gospel.

Children should understand the Jewish festival of Passover, as well as Jewish burial practices. For example, bodies were washed, anointed with oil and spices and wrapped in linen cloths. They were buried without delay, in the ground or in tombs cut from rock.

This assembly can be used before or after Easter, or to teach the story of the resurrection at any time of the year.

Bible references

Jesus is alive

MARK 16:1–11; JOHN 20:1–18

She thought he was the gardener and said, 'Sir, if you have taken his body away, please tell me, so I can go and get him.' Then Jesus said to her, 'Mary!' (John 20:15–16).

Discussion starters

Telling the truth

✢ Have you ever not been believed when you have told the truth? How did this make you feel?

✢ Why is it important to tell the truth?

✢ Do you think there is a link between telling the truth and trust?

Children may write their own poems or accounts of the story. The story can also be re-enacted or questions could be put to Mary in the hot seat, to investigate the feelings she may have had.

Visual demonstration

You will need: Small pottery jars, frankincense and myrrh (if available), Easter eggs

Show the children the small pottery jars and the frankincense and myrrh (if available). Explain that in biblical times, when someone died, their body would have been anointed with oil and special spices (frankincense and myrrh) and wrapped in linen cloth ready for burial. Show the Easter eggs. Ask the children why we give Easter eggs on Easter day. (*To celebrate new life and the stone rolled away from the tomb.*)

Introduction

Jesus' body was laid in a tomb provided by a man called Joseph of Arimathea, who was one of Jesus' disciples. Mary Magdalene planned to go to the tomb to anoint the body of Jesus with special oils and spices.

Eyewitness account: Mary Magdalene's story

I awoke early that morning after a night of fitful sleeping and dreaming. For a brief moment I lay still, dreams drifting through my mind. Suddenly, a wave of sorrow flooded my whole being as I recalled what my sleeping state had sought to obliterate. My Lord was dead. They had killed him. He had hung in pain. And yet, he seemed to know his fate, to embrace it with open arms, as he had embraced Judas, his betrayer.

What would we do now? Those who followed him were left bereft, without a purpose, a reason to live. Yet I knew that my Lord would want us to live: we all had a path to follow, until the end.

Although sorrow engulfed me, today I had a purpose. With the other women, I would go to the tomb to anoint his body with fragrant oils and spices. Such a small service for one so great and yet so humble—a king who would not wear a crown. They had mocked him with a purple robe and a crown of thorns, laughing as they called him 'King of the Jews'. Today we would give him reverence as a true king, our Lord and Messiah. My heart grew lighter with the thought of the special task ahead and I arose to prepare for the day. I wanted to take great care to prepare, for I would be in his presence.

The sun was hardly beginning to redden the sky when I met the other women and we walked out of the city to the place where the dead were buried. Our Lord had been laid to rest in the tomb of Joseph of Arimathea—a kind, gentle man, who had offered help with a saddened heart. Joseph had gone to Pilate to ask for Jesus' body. We women had watched as he was sealed inside the cave, noting the place so that we could find it again.

Walking silently, deep in thought, we were all still in a state of disbelief, wishing it had all been a bad dream, that someone would come to tell us we were mistaken. But no, we had seen his death with our own eyes—it was no fanciful tale but harsh reality. My reverie was suddenly broken by a thought.

'How will we get into the tomb?' I turned to my

companions, but they stared at me, slow to comprehend.

'The soldiers,' I explained. 'Pilate set his soldiers to stand guard, in case the disciples took Jesus' body away—and there's a huge boulder at the entrance. How will we get in?'

The other Mary smiled, trying to sound brave to reassure me.

'Well then, the soldiers will be there to help us to move the stone. Surely they have nothing to fear from a bunch of women coming to the tomb to anoint the body. Even Romans respect the dead.'

I agreed and felt much better. 'You're right, and we must go anyway. We must try.'

So on we went. As we neared the tomb, to our surprise we saw that the stone had been rolled away—but there were no soldiers to be seen. We went into the tomb and peered into the darkness. To our amazement, a young man in a white robe was sitting where Jesus' body had lain. We clung to each other in alarm, trembling with fear.

'Don't be alarmed!' said the young man. 'You are looking for Jesus from Nazareth, who was nailed to a cross. God has raised him to life, and he isn't here.'

Full of fear, we ran from the tomb. I ran to Simon Peter and told him what had happened. He and John leapt to their feet and rushed off to see for themselves. I returned to the tomb with them because I just did not know what to do. I was lost. My task of service could not be carried out, yet it was the only thing I had thought of. His body would not be prepared for rest now.

Peter and John were as amazed as we had been. First Peter and then John went into the empty tomb. They looked troubled and confused. Soon they left to return to the other disciples.

I stood alone, crying and trembling with despair. Where was he? What had they done with his body? Wasn't it enough that they had crucified him? Through my tears, I looked again at the cold stone. Suddenly, I was blinded by a light so bright that it was almost impossible to see. When I recovered my sight, I was amazed. Two angels sat where his body had lain, one at the head, the other at the feet.

'Why are you crying?' they asked.

'They have taken away my Lord's body! I don't know where they have put him.'

Just at that moment, something compelled me to turn round. There was a figure standing just a short way from me, his silhouette outlined against the rising sun. The gardener! He will know, I thought, resolving to approach him. He stepped forward, noticing my despair, and asked, 'Why are you crying?'

'Sir, if you have taken his body away, please tell me, so I can go and get him.'

He took another step towards me. 'Mary!' He spoke my name and I knew at once it was my Lord.

'Rabboni!' I answered, my heart filled with joy as I reached out to him.

'Don't hold on to me!' he said. 'But tell my disciples that I am going to the one who is my Father and my God, as well as your Father and your God.'

I ran to tell them: the Lord has risen! He has conquered death! But even though I had witnessed with my own eyes that Jesus was alive, they would not believe it.

Follow-up questions

Why were the women taking oils and spices to the tomb early on Sunday morning? Can you think of another time in the story of Jesus that we hear about frankincense and myrrh?

Suggested prayer

Dear Lord, thank you for the gift of your Son, Jesus Christ. His life was poured out to conquer death and show us the way to eternal life. Amen

Suggested songs

All in an Easter garden (*Come and Praise 2* 130)
Now the green blade rises (*Come and Praise 2* 131)
Alleluia, Alleluia, give thanks to the risen Lord (*Songs of Fellowship for Kids* 2)
This joyful Eastertide (*Junior Praise* 256)

Suggested music

'John 19:41' from *Jesus Christ Superstar* (to be played before the story is read at the start of the assembly)
'Hallelujah Chorus' from *Messiah* (G.F. Handel)
'I know that my Redeemer liveth' from *Messiah* (G.F. Handel)

Reflective poem: Mary's lament

Morning of sorrow,
Sad, tired footsteps.
My Lord gone,
Enclosed in a tomb.

Silent garden,
Why do birds sing?
My heart hangs heavy with loss.
Anointing his body,
Sacred, precious.

To assuage my grief,
Service to one
Who served all people:
The Lord's anointed Son.

Rock rolled, open tomb.
Sorrow to despair is given.
Scattered shroud,
No oils needed.
Sepulchre's cold stone.
He is gone!

Turned away in dull gloom,
No warmth in morning
sunlight,
Cave's cold shock numbs
feeling.

Forlorn garden tended.
Where have you taken him?
In pity, tell me.

'Mary!'

Rabboni! Teacher!
Sorrow fled,
Joyous, bright, blessed
morning!

He is risen!

Cleopas' story

Two disciples are walking on the road to Emmaus from Jerusalem, talking about the events leading to the crucifixion of Jesus. A stranger comes alongside them and asks them about their conversation. The stranger explains the meaning of the scriptures to them as they walk along. When they arrive at Emmaus, the stranger joins them for a meal. When he breaks the bread and gives a blessing, they realize with certainty that their travelling companion is Jesus, the risen Christ.

In his book *The Lord of the Rings: The Two Towers*, J.R.R. Tolkien describes a scene that echoes the story of the disciples' encounter with the risen Jesus on the road to Emmaus. This assembly compares Tolkien's story with Luke's account of Jesus' appearance on the road to Emmaus.

Read, or show from the film directed by Peter Jackson, the extract where Gandalf appears to Aragorn, Legolas and Gimli, disguised as an old man walking wearily and leaning on his staff. When the old man's rags draw apart, they realize that this is not Saruman as they had thought, but Gandalf, who has travelled through death after confronting the Balrog, and has emerged shining and clothed in white.

Bible references

MARK 16:12–13; LUKE 24:13–35

After Jesus sat down to eat, he took some bread. He blessed it and broke it. Then he gave it to them. At once they knew who he was, but he disappeared (Luke 24:30–31).

Discussion starters

Christian allegory

✣ In what ways do the stories in Luke's Gospel and Tolkien's book differ? In what ways are they the same?

Follow-up

Gandalf has changed and is not recognized at first. In comparison, Jesus is not recognized until he blesses and breaks bread as he did at the last supper. Both stories are accounts of resurrection from death in order to inspire and lead others. The emphasis is on rising from death, not just surviving without death having occurred.

Point out that J.R.R. Tolkien is telling a story, whereas the biblical account is real. Tolkien may well have taken his inspiration for his story from the account of Jesus' appearance on the road to Emmaus. Compare and contrast the fictitious story and the biblical account.

PSHE and Citizenship links

Look at the topic of change. Discuss the way in which we change at particular times of our lives—for example, during the transition to a new school or locality. We are also continuously changing and developing our personalities. Every day presents new opportunities to become a better person.

National Framework for RE links

Recognizing Christ in others: when we see qualities such as compassion, pity, kindness, forgiveness and mercy in others, Christians believe that we are able to recognize the risen Christ and his living message.

Visual demonstration

You will need: A staff or walking stick, some bread, a picture such as *The Supper at Emmaus* by Caravaggio (available on the National Gallery website: www.nationalgallery.org.uk)

Hold up the staff or walking stick and explain to the children that the assembly today is about a journey. Show the children the bread and tell them to listen closely to see why bread is part of today's story.

Introduction

Soon after Jesus had died, two of his disciples set out from Jerusalem to walk to the village of Emmaus. They were talking about the dreadful events that had taken place. This is the story of what happened to them, told by Cleopas.

Eyewitness account: Cleopas' story

Two of us were walking to Emmaus, a village outside Jerusalem. Our feet were heavy on the dusty road, weighed down by the grief in our hearts. The Lord was dead. They had taken him and crucified him with robbers, nailed to a cross under a sign mocking him as the king of the Jews.

What could we do now? What sort of followers were we, hiding away in fear? Our sorrow was mingled with guilt that we had not stood alongside him when they had arrested him—that we had left him to die on his own. Now we were filled with panic and confusion. How could we carry on? Our lives were empty and filled with shame. We had failed him.

We walked at first in silence and then started to put our pain into words. We were so engrossed in our shared sorrow, as we recollected the terrible events that had taken place over the festival of Passover, that we did not notice a man walking alongside us. Our slow pace must have allowed him to catch us up on the road.

He matched his pace to ours and we walked along easily with the stranger, feeling no fear, even though the road was lonely. After a while, the man spoke.

'What were you talking about as you walked along?'

I was astonished. 'Are you the only person in Jerusalem who doesn't know what happened there?' I replied with harsh disbelief.

'What do you mean?' he asked.

He seemed not to be offended by our attitude as, with some impatience and with growing anger and emotion, we explained what had happened to Jesus—how he had been arrested, tried and crucified, even though he had done nothing but good. We told him of our hope that Jesus would be the one to set Israel free from the oppression of Roman rule, and we shared with him our grief that it was not to be. And now, we explained, his tomb lay empty, the body gone. The women were talking of angels and saying he was alive.

We were so confused and upset as we poured out our story, but the stranger listened with calm patience to our ravings. When we had finished, he surprised us by saying, 'Why can't you understand? How can you be so slow to believe all that the prophets said? Didn't you know that the

Messiah would have to suffer before he was given his glory?'

We walked as if in a trance as he explained the words of the prophets written in the ancient scriptures. For the first time, I understood why God's Son came to earth, why he died so cruelly, and how this was the beginning, not the end. My despair turned to hope, flooding my whole being and filling my heart with warm gratitude. I could understand his purpose at last!

We arrived at Emmaus in no time, or so it seemed. The man seemed to want to continue on the road. We did not ask where he was going but begged him to come into the village with us. We wanted to hear more wisdom from this fascinating stranger who had lifted our sorrow and brought light back into our darkened lives.

He paused a moment, in deep thought, but agreed to come with us. We were glad to be able to offer him food and rest in return for his words on the road. He sat at the table with us and, straight away, took the bread in his hands. He raised it in thanks to God, broke it and shared it with us. All at once, we knew who he was. This was indeed our Lord Jesus. His face shone with smiling radiance as light filled the room surrounding him, brighter and brighter until we could not look at him. We turned our faces from the light, looked back and he was gone.

He has come back to us. In our despair, he has filled our hearts with renewed joy, light and love. Even at this late hour there is no time to lose: we cannot wait to return to Jerusalem to share our news with those who loved the Lord.

Follow-up questions

Ask if there has ever been a time when the children have not recognized someone, perhaps because they haven't seen the person for a long time, or because he or she was dressed differently or not in the place where the children would expect to see him or her. Ask them if they know why, in the story, the bread helped someone to be recognized.

Suggested prayer

Dear Lord, please help us to recognize you in those around us. Help us to see joy, kindness and concern. Help us also to let your love shine through our eyes. In Jesus' name. Amen

Suggested songs

I serve a risen Saviour (*Junior Praise* 113)
I met Jesus at the crossroads (*Junior Praise* 102)
I want to walk with Jesus Christ (*Junior Praise* 124)
I have decided to follow Jesus (*Songs of Fellowship for Kids* 79)

Suggested music

'The White Rider' from *The Lord of the Rings: The Two Towers* (Howard Shore)

Reflective poem: Breaking bread

In despair, walking.
Sharing sorrow,
Treading blindly the path.
Shattered strength
In grief, bowed.
Heads hanging.

In surprise, seeing.
Quiet questions.
Travelling lightly the way.
Soothing stranger
In company, restored.
Minds learning.

In friendship, eating.
Bread broken.
Bright shining light;
God's glory.
Life's resurrection, believed.
Heart's healing.

Reflective poem: Stranger on the road

Who is the stranger?
Walking the lonely road from Jerusalem.
Seemingly no knowledge of the terrible tragedy,
God's Son crucified,
Nailed to a cross,
Black night shrouding hope.

Who is the stranger?
Asking quiet questions on the road to Emmaus.
Peacefully explaining lessons of the scriptures.
Distance passed,
Stay with us,
Red sunset awakens hope.

Who is the stranger?
Breaking bread at the house in Emmaus.
Blessing as at the last supper.
Risen Lord in flesh,
Recognized Saviour,
White light grants hope.

Thomas' story

Jesus' disciple Thomas isn't present when Jesus first appears to the disciples in the locked room. Is it jealousy that leads him to demand first-hand experience of his risen Lord? Jesus knows Thomas' thoughts and demonstrates that true faith believes without seeing.

The material is designed to be used at the start of the summer term, but could be used at any time to discuss the issue of faith. Jesus' words, 'The people who have faith in me without seeing me are the ones who are really blessed!' are particularly significant. The story is followed by a reflective poem based on Jesus' words.

Bible references

Jesus and Thomas

JOHN 20:19–29

Jesus said, 'Thomas, do you have faith because you have seen me? The people who have faith in me without seeing me are the ones who are really blessed!' (v. 29).

What Jesus' followers must do

MATTHEW 28:16–20; MARK 16:14–18; LUKE 24:36–49

'Go to the people of all nations and make them my disciples. Baptize them in the name of the Father, the Son, and the Holy Spirit' (Matthew 28:19).

Discussion starters

Faith

✣ What does it mean to have faith in something?
✣ What things do you have faith in?
✣ What does it mean to be cynical?

Follow-up

Think about everyday things that we need to have faith in, such as the chair we sit on, the buildings we live and work in, the utilities that come into our homes and schools, the transport we use to travel, and so on. Why do we have faith in these everyday things? Is it important to have faith not just in everyday things, but in everyday life? Without faith, do you think we would be cynical? Do you think that today's society can sometimes be viewed in this way? If so, why?

PSHE and Citizenship links

Perhaps Thomas felt that he had been excluded from the experience of seeing the risen Jesus the first time. This could explain his reaction. Can pupils relate to these feelings? What problems can this cause?

Visual demonstration

You will need: A blindfold, a picture of doubting Thomas

For the picture, you could use *The Incredulity of Saint Thomas* by Caravaggio, or the picture of Jesus and Thomas in *The Life of Jesus through the Eyes of an Artist* (see page 125 for details).

Blindfold a pupil and ask if they can see anything. Hold up a book and ask if they can see it. Ask if they believe that you really are holding a book. How do they know whether or not you are?

After this demonstration, explain to the children that we can't see the air around us and yet we know it is there.

Introduction

Go on to explain that the assembly today is about Jesus' friend Thomas, who refused to believe that Jesus had risen from the dead unless he saw for himself.

Eyewitness account: Thomas' story

'We've seen the Lord. He was with us.' Andrew rushed towards me in excitement.

'What do you mean?' I looked at him blankly, puzzled.

'He came to see us in this very room. It was wonderful. You should have been here.'

'You're all upset, disturbed. You've been hiding away for too long. Now you're seeing ghosts.' I stared at them, wondering if their fear had caused them to lose their sanity.

They were desperately clinging to hope for the future when I could only see black despair.

'Jesus was not a ghost, Thomas. He was as solid as you or me. I could reach out my hand and touch him just as I can touch you!' He slapped my back with his hand.

'Have faith and believe, Thomas. Rejoice with us. He has risen from the dead.'

'What madness is this? Have you lost your minds?' I still refused to accept their wild words.

'It's not madness. He knew before it all happened. I'm sure he knew. It's as if it was planned.' Andrew's gaze was steady. He was determined to persuade me that he was telling the truth.

'I will not believe unless I touch the holes in his hands where the nails were. I have not seen him. I will not believe unless I have the proof of my own eyes.'

I tried to appear as controlled and calm as Andrew was, although I could feel myself starting to shake with anger. Why were they so sure when I had so many doubts?

I don't know why I refused to take Andrew's word that Jesus had risen. Perhaps I felt excluded. Why hadn't the Master appeared to me? I was one of the chosen. Had I failed him?

To be honest, I have to admit that my doubts were tinged with jealousy. When the others talked about seeing Jesus, I took myself aside, refusing to accept their joy and belief in the risen Lord. I convinced myself that they were deluded, overcome with grief; but in my heart, bitter sadness combined with anger and isolation.

My friends did not show any resentment towards me, but their joy and constant conversation about the risen Lord seemed like a judgment upon my refusal to believe.

A week later, we were all together once again. We had locked and bolted the door for fear of the Roman, or Jewish, authorities. We trusted no one. We were talking fearfully about events in Jerusalem. 'Are we safe here?' I asked, checking the door a second time, listening for footsteps that would herald our discovery. Suddenly, I was aware that the Lord was in our midst. He was as real and alive as—well, as you and me. He greeted us all, but he turned straight to me.

'Thomas,' he said. 'Put your finger here and look at my hands! Put your hand into my side. Stop doubting and have faith!'

I fell to my knees. 'You are my Lord and my God,' I said, distraught that I had not believed. Would he forgive me? How could I have doubted that he would return? Now I have seen him with my own eyes!

I looked up, seeking his face. His eyes pierced deep into my heart as he looked at me with sadness.

'Thomas, do you have faith because you have seen me? The people who have faith in me without seeing me are the ones who are really blessed!'

I knew that he was right. My jealous pride had stopped me from rejoicing and declaring my faith in him. I should have known that he would come to me when he judged that the time was right. Had he waited because he knew that I lacked faith? If so, I had been tested and I had failed him. The remembrance of that day would remain with me for the rest of my life.

Follow-up questions

❖ Why do you think Thomas would not believe the others when they told him they had seen Jesus?

❖ How would you have reacted if you had been Thomas?

Suggested prayer

Risen Lord, help us to have faith that you will always be with us on the journey of life—our guide in good and troubled times. Amen

Suggested songs

I'm gonna walk by faith (*Songs of Fellowship for Kids* 89)
To God be the glory! Great things he has done (*Junior Praise* 259)

Suggested music

'Jesu, joy of man's desiring' (J.S. Bach)

Reflective poem: Belief

What is belief?
To see is to know.
But to believe?
A deep feeling,
Unshakeable,
In your very being.
A knowing,
Soul felt.
Faith.

The scientific age,
Explaining all.
Can we still believe?
Find wonder?
Accept ignorance.
A knowing,
Soul felt.
Faith.

To reach beyond the material,
Build a bridge to God.
Those who have faith
But have not seen
Are most blessed.
A knowing,
Soul felt.
Faith.

Peter's story (2)

A short while after the disciples have met the risen Jesus, they seem to take comfort in the familiar: they decide to go fishing. Perhaps the suggestion, which came from Peter, was an attempt to get back to normal after the upheaval of the past three years and the traumatic events of the past three weeks. They go out in their boat and fish through the night, but they don't catch a single thing.

Early the next morning, Jesus appears to them and tells them where to catch fish. He cooks the fish and, there on the beach, eats with them, proving again that he is more than just a ghost. Peter's friendship is renewed and his life transformed when he experiences Jesus' forgiveness after his earlier denial.

This assembly shows how Peter received forgiveness from Jesus after he had denied him three times following Jesus' arrest. The story is followed by a choice of three reflective poems about forgiveness and friendship. The assembly can be used in conjunction with Unit 6 (see pages 50–58). Equally, the material can be used on its own early in the summer term as part of work on the resurrection.

Bible references

Jesus appears to seven disciples

JOHN 21:1–19

Jesus asked a third time, 'Simon son of John, do you love me?' Peter was hurt because Jesus had asked him three times if he loved him. So he told Jesus, 'Lord, you know everything. You know I love you.' Jesus replied, 'Feed my sheep' (v. 17).

Discussion starters

Forgiveness

✣ If someone forgives you, what do you need to do in response?
✣ Which is easier, to forgive someone else or to forgive yourself?

Follow-up

When Jesus forgave Peter, Peter became the rock on which the Christian Church was founded. Pupils may discuss our ability to forgive others and also to seek forgiveness for things that we have done wrong.

National Framework for RE links

Asking God for forgiveness for things that we have done wrong or good things we have failed to do is an important part of the discussion in Religious Education. The request for God's mercy can be seen within the service of Holy Communion, where Christians follow the instructions given by Jesus at the last supper.

Visual demonstration

You will need: A fishing net, photographs of the Sea of Galilee (Lake Tiberias)

Ask the children how they feel when they have tried really hard to do something but haven't had any success. This is the way the disciples felt when they went fishing on Lake Tiberias (another name for Lake Galilee). Show the picture of the Sea of Galilee (Lake Tiberias). Hold up the fishing net and explain that shortly after the disciples had met the risen Jesus, they decided to go fishing. They spent the whole night trying to catch some fish, but without success. By morning they were feeling very tired and despondent.

Introduction

Many of Jesus' disciples had been fishermen before giving up their jobs to become followers of Jesus as he went from town to town telling people about God. In this story, Peter tells us what happened when they went fishing after Jesus' death and resurrection.

Eyewitness account: Peter's story (2)

So many amazing things had happened since the days in Jerusalem. Time had passed so quickly, the days filled from sunrise to sunset.

We had been travelling and found ourselves by the familiar shores of Lake Galilee—the Romans call it Lake Tiberias. As we sat talking one evening, I looked across at the water, still and unfathomable like the soul. The lake seemed to be calling to me and I knew I had to find a boat, to return to the roots of my being.

'I'm going fishing!' I announced to the others. To my surprise, they were filled with enthusiasm.

'Ah, fish for breakfast! What a splendid idea!' laughed James.

'I know a man who will lend us his boat, I'm sure,' added Nathanael.

'Well, Peter,' grinned John, slapping me on the back, 'we could hardly let you go alone!'

So it was agreed. The promise of a breakfast of freshly caught fish was stronger than the draw of our beds and we set out across the lake. At first we were in good humour, despite the hour. Many of us were fishermen before following the Lord and the natural rhythm of the water recalled idyllic days of our lives when fishermen were all we had been.

'What will we do with the fish we don't eat?' someone asked.

'Well, I'm pretty hungry!' laughed James. 'But seriously, there's a village not far away. I'm sure we'll find people in need.'

It was a good feeling, producing food for others, when so many had kept us fed through kindness and support for our work.

Gradually, our satisfaction evaporated. Where were the fish? True, I could remember poor nights' work in the past but, with such high hopes, I couldn't believe it would happen now. The laughter died down, although at first we were slow to complain, clinging to our dreams of success. One by one, we gave in to despair. We had failed: our hopes of breakfast with food to spare for those in need evaporated like the morning mists, along with our idyllic memories of the fisherman's life.

We agreed to give up and make for the shore. As we came nearer, we could see someone standing, looking out across the water. A solitary figure, still at first and then waving a greeting.

'Who's that?' asked Nathanael.

'I don't know, but I hope he doesn't want fish,' I replied, annoyed that we had a witness to our lack of success. The man shouted out to us, 'Friends, have you caught anything?' We had to admit we hadn't.

'Let your net down on the right side of the boat and you will catch some fish.'

Anything was worth a try—our last attempt before going back to shore. We put the nets down into the water, which was starting to reflect the early morning sun. I remember thinking it was a little late to catch anything now that dawn was breaking.

How wrong I was! The nets were soon heavy with fish, so heavy that we could hardly move them.

John called out in excitement, 'It's the Lord!'

Immediately, I gathered my robes about me and jumped into the water. I wanted to be the first to get to him. When I got to the shore, I saw that Jesus had made a fire. The aroma of fish barbecuing over charcoal filled my nostrils. Bread was ready to complete the meal.

'Bring some of the fish you have just caught,' Jesus said, smiling at our delight.

I scrambled back into the boat and helped to bring in the catch: 153 large fish. An amazing success! The Lord invited us to come and eat. He gave out bread and cooked fish, so that again we shared a meal together. How unlike that night in the upper room at Jerusalem!

When we had finished eating, Jesus said to me, 'Simon, son of John, do you love me more than the others do?'

I answered, 'Yes, Lord, you know I do!'

He replied, 'Then feed my lambs.'

He continued, 'Simon, son of John, do you love me?'

I answered again, 'Yes, Lord, you know I love you.'

'Then take care of my sheep,' he said.

Again Jesus asked, 'Simon, son of John, do you love me?'

I had denied him three times and he had questioned me thrice. I was deeply hurt but managed to speak. 'Lord, you know everything. You know I love you.'

He looked at me with a steady gaze. 'Feed my sheep.'

In this way, I knew I was forgiven for having denied knowing him. He said, 'Follow me!'

I couldn't wait to begin!

Follow-up questions

✢ Can you think of another time when Jesus had helped his disciples to bring in a catch of fish?

✢ Why do you think Jesus asked Peter three times if he loved him?

✢ What did Jesus mean when he said, 'Feed my sheep'?

Suggested prayer

Dear Lord, you can see into our hearts and you know our deepest thoughts. Help us to trust in your mercy, forgive us when we do wrong and help us to forgive others as you forgive us. Amen

Suggested songs

Yours be the glory, risen, conquering Son (*Junior Praise* 299)
There's new life in Jesus, lift up your heart (*Junior Praise* 249)

Suggested music

'Out of the deep (Psalm 130)' from *Requiem* (John Rutter)
'Benedictus' from *The Armed Man* (Karl Jenkins)

Reflective poem: On the shore

Water glistens,
Reflecting life past.
Into the deep
Our nets are cast.

Time passes.
Nothing there.
Failure to fish
Fuels our despair.

Figure hails
Friends from the shore.
Cast your nets,
Catch more and more.

Food cooks,
Fish and bread.
By his hands
Our lives are led.

Words spoken,
Simon, son of John,
Questioning my love,
Telling me, 'Carry on.'

Feed my sheep,
He who knows all.
Follow me,
Again heed my call.

Reflective poem: Morning meeting

Early morning mist
Drifts along the shore.
Shining light
Breaks through.

Reflection of reality,
He is here.
Ethereal presence,
Risen life: God with us.

White sand,
Feet hot on firm ground,
Standing with us.
Sharing food, as before.

The Son of Man,
Showing God's love.
Forgiveness and friendship,
Sealed with the symbol of fish.

Reflective poem: Follow me

Water glistens,
Reflecting past life.
Nets cast deep,
Failure, despair,
No fish.

Figure on the shore
Hails friends,
Full catch on his advice,
Sharing food.
The Lord is here!

Bread and fish
By his own hand.
Questioning thrice.
Memories of the night
Watching in despair.

Take care of lambs,
Feed the sheep,
Guide believers,
As did the shepherd.
Go forward; follow.

Death of honour,
God decreed,
Following the Master.
Held in old age
Through pain, to glory.

I am forgiven.

Matthew's story

The setting for this assembly is the village of Bethany, which was on the slopes of the Mount of Olives. The risen Jesus has taken the initiative in leading the disciples to the place from which he will return finally to his heavenly Father. The ascension combines a sense of continued companionship with that of loss and, perhaps, confusion. What will happen next?

The assembly should be used at Ascension. It can be combined with a discussion about pupils' views and beliefs about heaven. The use of art depicting the ascension can help this study. The story is followed by reflective poetry, exploring questions about heaven. What is it and what is it like?

Bible references

Jesus returns to heaven

MARK 16:19–20; LUKE 24:50–53; ACTS 1:1–13

Jesus led his disciples out to Bethany, where he raised his hands and blessed them. As he was doing this, he left and was taken up to heaven (Luke 24:50–51).

Discussion starters

Sadness and loss

✤ How would it feel if your best friend moved away to another country and you never saw them again?

✣ What things would remind you of them?
✣ How would you keep in touch?

Follow-up

Research the story in *The Lord of the Rings: The Return of the King* when Frodo, Bilbo and Gandalf leave for the Grey Havens at the end of their adventures. They say goodbye to Sam, Merry and Pippin, having formed deep friendships and endured so much together. As you did with the story of the road to Emmaus, discuss the Christian allegory that J.R.R. Tolkien has used in his storyline.

PSHE and Citizenship links

Children can discuss the disciples' feelings when Jesus finally left them to return to his heavenly Father. Compare how they would have felt at the horror and trauma of the crucifixion with how they might have felt at the ascension. Consider the sense of loss and grief when someone dies and the feeling of sadness when saying goodbye to someone who is moving away and may not be seen again.

Visual demonstration

You will need: A picture of the ascension, such as the one by Giotto di Bondone or Tintoretto (see page 125 for details)

Ask the children if they have ever said goodbye to someone, knowing that they might never see them again (such as when a friend moves away to another country). How does it feel to think you may never see that person again? Show a picture of the ascension and explain that the disciples must have felt a great sense of sadness and loss when the risen Jesus finally returned to his heavenly Father.

Introduction

Explain that the disciples were with Jesus when he was taken up to heaven. Our story today is told by Jesus' close friend Matthew, who was one of the disciples with Jesus at the time of the ascension.

Eyewitness account: Matthew's story

Jesus was with us many times after the miracle of his resurrection. He walked with us, talked with us and ate with us. Without his presence among us, we would have been inconsolable after his death. How amazing that he was there! He had told us that we were to carry on telling people about God, just as he had done. We now had a new message to add—that Jesus, God's own Son, had conquered death and opened the kingdom of heaven to all who believed. Such news! But we were to stay in Jerusalem until God sent us the power to carry his message.

The day came when he spoke to us with some sadness in his deep brown eyes.

'My friends, the time has come. I must leave you and return to my Father. He will send his Holy Spirit to be with you when I am gone.'

John turned to him with tears in his eyes. 'Master, we thought we had lost you for ever, but you came back to us. Is it written that we must grieve again?'

Jesus smiled, 'No, John, this time there is no grief, only joy. I am going home, to the place where you will join me when your time comes. My work is done but yours is just beginning. Take heart—you have much to accomplish, my brothers. Come with me today. We will go to Bethany so that you can witness my return to heaven.'

We went out of the city. Bethany was less than three kilometres from Jerusalem, the scene of many great adventures in our lives with Jesus. The little village nestles in the foothills of the Mount of Olives. We climbed a little way up.

'Stay here,' the Lord instructed us as he turned to continue on his way.

Once more looking back towards us, he smiled the deep, warm smile that filled us with peace. I felt a strange warmth around my heart and a feeling of love for all creation.

'God bless you, my friends. I will always be with you, even though you will not be able to see me.'

He turned away and continued a little further up the hill. We could see him clearly as he closed his eyes and offered a prayer to heaven with outstretched arms. Suddenly, the blue sky filled with cloud, shrouding the hill on which we stood. All at once, we could not see the Master clearly, yet a white, shining light was breaking through the cloud, almost blinding us as we tried to see where he was.

All too soon, the light dimmed and the cloud started to clear, but he was gone. In his place stood two men, dressed in white clothes. They said, 'Why are you men from Galilee standing here and looking up into the sky? Jesus has been taken to heaven. But he will come back in the same way that you have seen him go.'

It was as if we had woken from a dream. We shook ourselves awake and stumbled down the hill, too amazed to talk of the evidence of our own eyes.

Together we returned to Jerusalem, to the upstairs room where we had been staying. I was filled with a deep sense of peace and love. The warmth in my heart stayed with me as I sat thinking about everything that had happened since I became a follower of Jesus. We said little to one another about that day, drawn together by prayer and the task ahead. How were we to continue the work begun by our dear Lord? How would we make ourselves worthy of the task entrusted to us?

Follow-up questions

In what ways was Jesus' disappearance at the ascension different from his disappearance after breaking bread with the two disciples in Emmaus? What was the work that Jesus wanted his disciples to accomplish?

Suggested prayer

Dear Lord, thank you for sending Jesus to live among us. By his example he showed us how to live our lives. May our lives be worthy of him. Amen

Suggested songs

Lord, we come in adoration (*Songs of Fellowship for Kids* 124)
Lord, I lift your name on high (*Songs of Fellowship for Kids* 119)
Who took fish and bread, hungry people fed? (*Junior Praise* 286)

Suggested music

'O be joyful in the Lord' (John Rutter)
'O how glorious is the kingdom' (Basil Harwood)
'The Grey Havens' and 'Into the West' from *The Lord of the Rings: The Return of the King* (Howard Shore)

Reflective poem: Ascension

Earthly presence   *Flight of sorrow*
Taken in death   *Turned to joy*
Nailed to a cross   *Cloud obscured*
Laid in a cold tomb   *Christ ascended*

Risen Lord
Returned among us
Master, friend
Son of God

Reflective poem: Heaven

What would you want of heaven?
Eternal idleness?
Clouds, harps?
Would this be heaven?

Timeless bliss?
Life sentence?
Think hard.
What would be your heaven?

Eternal peace?
Everlasting love?
All-seeing knowledge?
Useful occupation?

When can the soul
Complete its journey?
Merge with God,
Be worthy?

At the end of a life,
How many of us
Are friends of God,
Ready for heaven?

Philip's story

The story explores our understanding of the Trinity (God the Father, Jesus the Son and God the Holy Spirit) and the coming of the Holy Spirit at Pentecost. It explains how the disciples were given power from God to spread the good news of Jesus and become the founders of the Christian Church.

The assembly can be used at Pentecost or at any time to explore the development of the Christian Church. The material also lends itself to discussions about peer pressure—what it means not to follow the crowd and to be your own person. The story is followed by a news report about how, after the coming of the Holy Spirit, the disciples speak to crowds about Jesus.

Bible references

The coming of the Holy Spirit

ACTS 2:1–47

The Holy Spirit took control of everyone, and they began speaking whatever languages the Spirit let them speak (Acts 2:4).

Discussion starters

Peer pressure

✢ What do we mean by the term 'peer pressure'?
✢ Is it easier to follow the crowd or to be your own person?

Follow-up

The ability to make decisions as an individual instead of following the crowd can be discussed. The events of Pentecost caused the disciples to set themselves against the established society of their day. Have pupils write their own reports of the events of Pentecost, or record or film interviews which describe the scene. Hot-seat a disciple or onlooker in the crowd. Alternatively, role-play what happened to the disciples at Pentecost and the response of the crowd. In what ways did the disciples go against the grain of their society?

The material also provides an opportunity to explore the use of a mandala as an aid to Christian meditation. Mandalas are universal images. They occur abundantly in nature, and can be found in rose windows in cathedrals and other forms of sacred art. They are widely used in Tibetan and Indian cultures, as well as by North American Indians. They are often used for meditation and healing. Modern designs can be incorporated into mandalas to show the Christian symbols present at Pentecost, such as flames, wind and different languages.

PSHE and Citizenship links

The disciples were changed by the coming of the Holy Spirit and their lives had a new purpose. The summer term is a time in the year when older Key Stage 2 children are preparing for the move to secondary school, with the changes that this involves. Therefore, this form of change can be discussed following this assembly.

National Framework for RE links

The unit introduces discussion about the work of the early Church and the spread of the good news of Jesus. The story of Peter's forgiveness when he met Jesus on the beach is also relevant (see Unit 12 on pages 93–100).

Visual demonstration

> **You will need:** Words from different languages written out (or an audio recording of languages), a picture of the Day of Pentecost

For the picture, use 'The coming of the Holy Spirit' from *The Life of Jesus through the Eyes of an Artist* (see page 125 for details).

Show the children the words and ask if they know what they mean. Alternatively, play the audio recording and ask if they understand what is being said. Ask pupils to put their hands up if they would like to be able to speak to everyone in the world in their own language. Explain that today's assembly is about how Jesus' disciples were able to tell lots of different people about Jesus.

Introduction

After Jesus had returned to his heavenly Father, his disciples were together in Jerusalem, waiting and praying as Jesus had asked them to do. It was the time of the festival of Pentecost, so Jerusalem would have been full of people visiting the city to celebrate harvest.

Eyewitness account: Philip's story

Just before his ascension to heaven, Jesus had told us to wait in Jerusalem for the coming of God's Holy Spirit—and this we did, although we little knew what to expect. It was the time of the festival of Pentecost, when many people come into our great city for the harvest celebrations. At that time, many of us who followed Jesus met together, talking of our plans to carry on telling people about God and the good news of Jesus, now that he had returned to heaven. At a guess, there were about 120 of us, including the women and Jesus' family—his mother Mary, and his brothers. It was quite a gathering!

'We need to get out and about if we are to tell people about Jesus,' said John. 'There's no good in hiding away together. You know what our Lord said about putting a light under a bowl—it's not much use!'

Bartholomew sighed, 'Well, I don't know how much use I'll be, travelling around. People won't be able to understand me, or I them.'

'You are right,' agreed John. 'We need people who speak the languages of each place. This news must be spread far and wide.'

Suddenly, there was a noise like a mighty wind, which filled the house. We looked around with startled faces, not knowing what to do. Was heaven angered by our lack of faith? There was nowhere to run or hide. Our ears were filled with noise like the power of a great wind whistling around us. Instinctively, we ducked our heads, but when we looked up we saw what looked like flames, dividing into fiery tongues and resting on each person in that room.

I grasped John's hand and we all joined together, hand clinging to hand, and waited for God's will. I saw a fiery tongue settle on Peter's head and then I, too, felt the amazing power of God's Spirit running like fire and water through my very being. I can't describe the feeling of pure joy that flooded through me as I became filled with the Holy Spirit, just as the Lord had promised. We fell to our knees, hands reaching out, and then prostrate on the floor, marvelling at the power that surged through our bodies.

James began to speak, praising the Lord, and we all joined in with him. Whatever words came from his mouth, we understood and added our voices to his. We must have been making a terrible noise because there was a banging on the door and, when John rushed to open it, we saw a crowd outside, come to listen to the commotion and find out what was going on.

Peter rushed out and we all followed him. We spoke to individuals within the crowd and, amazingly, each person understood us! There were people from many different countries in the city that day—people from Parthia, Media, Elam, Egypt, Crete, Arabia and many others from far away. A buzz of excitement raced through the crowd as they realized that they were hearing us praise God, each in his or her own language. But even then, many did not want to believe.

'They must be drunk!' someone shouted.

'What is going on?' asked another. 'What does it mean?'

Peter stepped forward and spoke to the crowd.

'You are wrong to think that these people are drunk. It is only nine o'clock in the morning. Who can show me a bar open at this time?'

They laughed nervously and he went on, quoting the scriptures as he spoke.

'God led the prophet Joel to say, "I will give my Spirit to everyone and they will prophesy."'

He then went on to tell them about Jesus and his triumph over death. The people were afraid when he told them that they had put God's Son to death on a cross. Their eyes filled with fear and they looked to heaven as though they expected to be struck down at that very moment.

'What shall we do?' they cried out.

Peter told them, 'Turn back to God! Be baptized in the name of Jesus Christ, so that your sins will be forgiven.'

All day, they came forward. We prayed and baptized each person in the name of our Lord. Around 3000 people were received into God's family that day. We broke bread with them, just as Jesus had commanded us, and prayed together.

The message had been delivered. It had begun.

Follow-up questions

The coming of the Holy Spirit is likened to the sound of a mighty wind and the sight of fiery flames. What other symbols of the Holy Spirit do you know about? Why do you think Christians use symbols to describe the power of God?

Suggested prayer

Dear Lord, help us to be happy to come alongside people from all parts of your world. Fill our hearts with the love and power of your Holy Spirit and help us to know your Son, Jesus Christ. Amen

Suggested songs

Spirit of peace (*Come and Praise 2* 185)
Light up the fire (*Come and Praise 1* 55)
All over the world, the Spirit is moving (*Junior Praise* 5)

Suggested music

Te Deum (Charpentier)

Reflective news report: The Daily Israelite

The news report below can be read as a presentation piece in assembly. Pupils could also write their own reports dealing with this or any other event of the Easter story.

THE DAILY ISRAELITE

AD33 10 SHEKELS

PENTECOST HARVEST FOR NEW RELIGION

The crowds gathered in Jerusalem for the Pentecost celebrations got more than they bargained for yesterday when the disciples of Jesus of Nazareth were suddenly filled with a strange power.

Jesus was crucified earlier this year at the time of the festival of Passover. He was put to death for stirring up trouble and claiming to be the king of the Jews. After his death, there were rumours that he had risen from the grave, but everything has been pretty quiet since then. Now, some six weeks later, we have reports that there has been a disturbance at one of the houses in the city. Eyewitnesses from many countries claim to have heard Jesus' followers speaking in their very own languages.

One man said, 'At first we thought they were drunk, but, as one of them pointed out, it was only 9 o'clock in the morning!' It seems that Peter's insistence that they were not drunk, but filled with God's Holy Spirit, was true. The fisherman from Galilee spoke very powerfully, explaining all about Jesus' life and death and proving through scripture that Jesus was the Son of God.

As many as 3000 people have believed his message and joined ranks with the followers of Jesus. The sight of so many people asking for forgiveness and being baptized has never before been seen in the streets of our city.

Drunk or divine? Send your comments to our readers' page. There'll be a 100-shekel prize for the best comment.

Paul's story

We first meet Paul when he is known as Saul, a prominent persecutor of the followers of Jesus. We are told that he 'approved the stoning of Stephen', the first Christian martyr (Acts 8:1). Saul encountered the risen Christ when he was travelling from Jerusalem to Damascus. His conversion to the Christian faith and subsequent involvement in the early Church help children to understand how Christianity has been passed on down the years and how we, in our own time, are an important part of that journey of faith.

This assembly can be used in the summer term to explore the growth of the early Christian Church. It is important to emphasize that Saul was an enemy of those who followed Jesus. He was well known as someone who arrested Christians and flung them in jail. He was the most unlikely supporter of the Christian faith until he met the risen Christ. If someone like Saul can experience a complete reversal in his thinking and behaviour, then anything is possible.

The geographical and political context of the early Church gives plenty of scope for cross-curricular learning. For example, children can research Paul's journeys as he spread the news of Jesus across the known world. It is useful to examine maps to show the extent of Paul's journeys. Children may be surprised at some of the places he visited to establish Christian communities.

Bible references

Saul becomes a follower of the Lord

ACTS 9:1–24; 22:6–16; 26:12–18

'Who are you?' Saul asked. 'I am Jesus,' the Lord answered. 'I am the one you are so cruel to. Now get up and go into the city, where you will be told what to do' (Acts 9:5–6).

Discussion starters

Thinking and behaviour

✣ Have you ever changed your mind about something so completely that you started acting quite differently?

✣ What made you change, and what difference did it make to your life?

Follow-up

Create a role-play to re-enact Paul's conversion. Write poems describing the events on the road, including Paul's blindness, his recovery and the change in his thinking and behaviour. Use art materials to design interlocking hands and eyes, showing the importance of reaching out to others and seeing things around us with truth and faith. You may wish to create a mandala design using these ideas.

PSHE and Citizenship links

Talk about the ways that people express their Christian faith. What difference does faith make to a person's life? Paul's transformation from a persecutor of Jesus' followers to one of Christianity's greatest evangelists is an important aspect of the story of the Christian Church. Paul's new life shows that anything is possible. How might having a Christian faith make a difference to the way people think and behave?

Visual demonstration

You will need: Four children for a freeze-frame re-enactment of the moment when Saul met the risen Jesus on the road to Damascus

Choose one of your four volunteers to play the part of Saul as he is struck down by the brightness of the light. The other three volunteers play the soldiers who were accompanying Paul on the journey to Damascus. You will need to rehearse your volunteers ahead of the assembly so that they can take up their positions quickly and effectively.

Introduction

When the volunteers have got into their positions for the freeze-frame, begin the assembly by asking who the children would choose to help them to do something really important. Would they choose someone who was really nasty to them? Explain that after Jesus' death, his disciples were given the power of God's Holy Spirit to help them spread the news that Jesus was God's Son. As the Christian faith started to grow, some people were determined to wipe it out. Jesus chose someone who was determined to destroy all those who believed to become his greatest helper. Ask the children to look out for the place in the story that your volunteers are demonstrating in their freeze-frame. The volunteers can relax their positions while you tell the story.

Eyewitness account: Paul's story

'Troublemakers, blasphemers. I'm going to rid the world of them!'

I spoke strong words to the chief priests. It was a vow I had taken. My life's purpose was to bring to justice those who destroyed the true faith. Proudly, I thought of myself as a leader in the fight against the followers of Jesus of Nazareth. He had been put to death, crucified as a troublemaker who blasphemed the laws of God. Now his supporters, 'People of the Way' as they called themselves, were following him to the grave. They seemed filled with a new vigour since his death. His disciples were going about telling people that Jesus had risen from the grave and was the true Messiah. Such nonsense! But their teaching was adding to their number day by day. We had to stop the force of this movement. I was determined to succeed where others had failed.

My work took me far and wide in the search for my enemies—the enemies of the Jewish faith (as I saw them). I set out for the city of Damascus with letters from the high priest in Jerusalem, giving me authority to arrest any of those who claimed to believe in Jesus. I set out on the road with soldiers to aid my mission.

We made good time and I could see the city ahead. The sun was hot and we slowed our pace. We were still far outside the city when, suddenly, a great light filled the sky. It flashed around me, so bright that I fell to the ground in fear, hiding my eyes. The soldiers too were terrified and fell to the ground, trying to steady their horses as they shielded their eyes.

I shook with fear, but it became worse. A voice echoed around me: 'Saul, Saul, why are you so cruel to me?'

I struggled to find my voice, croaking my reply, 'Who are you?'

The voice answered, but I knew before I heard the words. 'I am Jesus. I am the one you are so cruel to. Now get up and go to the city, where you will be told what to do.'

The light was replaced by darkness. I tried to open my eyes, but something pressed on them. I felt with my hands— hard scales blocked my sight. I could not even cry the tears that burnt inside with bitter pain.

'I can't see.' My voice was angered, but muffled with confusion.

I felt a steady hand on my arm, and then another, helping me to stand.

'Did you see anyone?' I asked them.

'No, sir, there was no one, but we will take you into the city as you were commanded.' I could not see the faces of the soldiers, who must have been almost as shaken and nervous as I was myself.

I waited in Damascus. Day and night were the same—time was meaningless. I could not eat or drink.

What could Jesus want with me? Why had he not struck me dead? Perhaps I was to endure a slow torture, a dark night of the soul.

Eventually, there came a knock on the door of the house in Straight Street, which had been my prison and my refuge for the last three days. I felt my way, taking some time. My shaking hand opened the door. I knew in my heart that the time had come.

I felt warm, soft hands upon my face and a steady voice spoke to me: 'Saul, the Lord Jesus has sent me. He is the same one who appeared to you along the road. He wants you to see, and be filled with the Holy Spirit.'

Light flooded my being as the fish-like scales fell from my eyes. At first, a blurred shape, then the face of a man was before me as my sight returned.

'Thank you, my friend.' I spoke for the first time in days, but fell again to my knees. 'I know you must fear and hate me, but I am so unworthy. Help me in the name of the Lord Jesus.'

'It is as I am commanded, to do God's will.'

Ananias poured water into a bowl, gave thanks to God and made the sign of the cross on my forehead. 'I baptize you in the name of the Father, the Son and the Holy Spirit.'

There, my life started. Soon afterwards, I changed my Jewish name, Saul, to the Greek name of Paul. My heart burnt with a new fire. My life had a new purpose. This is the beginning of my story.

Follow-up questions

Why did Jesus choose Paul, who you might have thought would be the last person chosen to spread the gospel message? In what ways does Jesus' choice of Paul make the story more powerful?

Suggested prayer

Dear Lord, help us to hear you in the rush and noise of our daily lives. Help us to take time to be quiet and to hear your voice. Amen

Suggested songs

Amazing grace (*Junior Praise* 8)
At the name of Jesus (*Junior Praise* 13)
Christ triumphant, ever reigning (*Junior Praise* 25)

Suggested music

'Thy rebuke hath broken his heart' and 'Behold, and see if there be any sorrow' from *Messiah* (G.F. Handel)
'O man bemoan thy grievous sin' from *St Matthew Passion* (J.S. Bach)
'Te Deum' (Arvo Pärt)
'Sanctus' from *The Armed Man* (Karl Jenkins)

Reflective freeze-frame

Saul becomes a follower of the Lord

Ask your volunteers to re-form their freeze-frame. Choose a further four pupils to form a freeze-frame of the soldiers leading the blinded Paul into Damascus, one pupil to take the position of Paul waiting in the house in Straight Street and, finally, two pupils to take the positions of Ananias and Paul at the point where Paul's sight is restored. When all the children are in position, play some reflective music to give the children time to think about how the story is being demonstrated by the four freeze-frames.

Glossary of terms

Ascension: Jesus' return to heaven, forty days after the resurrection.

Baptism: A symbolic act (sacrament) using water: a religious ceremony in which Christians make a public confession that they have repented of their sins and committed themselves in faith to Jesus.

Blasphemy: To speak disrespectfully of God or sacred things.

Centurion: An officer in the Roman army, in charge of 100 soldiers.

Charlatan: A person falsely claiming a skill or profession.

Children of Israel: Name for the Israelites, who later became the Jewish nation.

Christian: A follower of Jesus Christ: a person who believes in the life, death and resurrection of Jesus Christ.

Creation story: A story to show that God is the creator of all things, visible and invisible.

Crucifixion: Method of execution by nailing or tying someone to a cross and leaving them to die.

David's son: The Messiah (Jesus) was descended from David, who was king of the Israelites around 1200BC. David was the shepherd boy who became Israel's second king. He was the founder of the royal line from which the Messiah was eventually born, the composer and collector of many of the Psalms and the person who slew the Philistine giant, Goliath.

Ethereal: Heavenly; spirit-like.

Faith: Trust or confidence in God without proof of sight.

Grim reaper: The personification of death.

Heaven: The dwelling place of God.

Holy City: Jerusalem.

Holy Communion: The sacrament in which Christians break bread and drink wine as instructed by Jesus at the last supper. Also known as the Eucharist, the Lord's Supper, or the Mass.

Holy Spirit: The third person of the Trinity, based on the doctrine that the Godhead comprises Father, Son and Holy Spirit; the power of God.

Legion: A body of 3000–6000 soldiers in ancient Rome.

Messiah: 'The anointed one' (Hebrew): the person chosen by God to free the people from oppression.

Mission: A particular task with a purpose, given to a person or group of people.

Money changers: Men changing shekels to special temple money to be used to buy sacrifices within the temple.

Nazarene: A person from the town of Nazareth.

Passover: Annual Jewish festival commemorating the exodus, when the

Israelites escaped from slavery in Egypt. The name comes from the time when the angel of death 'passed over' the homes of the Israelites because the doors of their houses were smeared with lamb's blood.

Pentecost: A word meaning '50', referring to the Israelite harvest festival 50 days after Passover. In the Old Testament, Pentecost is known as the feast of Harvest, the feast of Firstfruits and the feast of Weeks, which is the Jewish festival of *Shavuot*. God poured his Holy Spirit upon the first disciples on the day of Pentecost, showing that they were the firstfruits of the Church of Jesus Christ.

People of Israel: See Children of Israel.

Promised land: Canaan: the land God promised to Abraham and his descendants, lying between Sidon and Gaza on the Mediterranean coast and the River Jordan.

Prophecy: A message from God, telling people of God's will or foretelling the future.

Rabboni: A strengthened form of 'Rabbi', the Jewish word for a teacher.

Resurrection: The Christian belief that Jesus rose from the dead.

Sabbath: The Jewish day of rest; a holy day when no work should be done.

Sacrament: A Christian rite: a symbol of something spiritual and sacred.

Sacrifice: Practice of killing an animal and giving it as a burnt offering to God.

Sanctimonious: Hypocritical; falsely holy.

Satan: Hebrew for 'enemy'; the adversary of God; the devil.

Scriptures: The name given by the Jewish people to the Old Testament part of the Bible.

Shekel: Jewish coin.

Son of Man: Jesus' most common title for himself, signifying that he was both human and divine. The reference alludes to the vision in the book of Daniel: 'I saw what looked like a son of man coming with the clouds of heaven, and he was presented to the Eternal God. He was crowned king and given power and glory, so that all people of every nation and race would serve him. He will rule for ever, and his kingdom is eternal, never to be destroyed' (Daniel 7:13–14).

Spirit: The non-physical, moral and emotional essence of a person, based on the belief that a human being is made up of body, mind and spirit. A person's spirit is also known as the soul.

Temple: The house of God in Jerusalem: the most important building in the Jewish religion.

Terrorist: A person who uses violence or intimidating behaviour against a government or community for political gain.

Bibliography

Books

+ The Bible: Contemporary English Version, published by Harper-Collins. To ensure that the full meaning of the original is always made clear, the CEV translates each sentence or idea rather than each word on its own. This gives it a clarity that is easy to read and understand and ideal for reading aloud.
+ Religious Education: The non-statutory national framework published by the Qualifications and Curriculum Authority (QCA)
+ The National Curriculum published by the Department for Education and Employment (DFEE) and QCA
+ A scheme of work for Key Stage 1 and 2: Religious Education published by QCA
+ *Easter in Art*, Tim Marlow, a Seventh Art production for Channel Five (2003)
+ *The Christian Faith and its Symbols*, Jan Thompson, Edward Arnold (1996)
+ *The Complete Bible Handbook*, John Bowker, Dorling Kindersley (2004)
+ *Teaching Christian Citizenship*, Gaynor Cobb, Kevin Mayhew Ltd (2003)
+ *Living Easter through the Year*, John Pritchard, SPCK (2005)

Music books

+ *Come and Praise 1* (BBC Education)
+ *Come and Praise 2* (BBC Education)
+ *Songs of Fellowship for Kids* (Kingsway Music)
+ *Junior Praise* (HarperCollins)
+ *Someone's Singing, Lord* (A&C Black)

Art

❖ *Christ Driving the Traders from the Temple,* El Greco (National Gallery, London)

❖ *The Sacrament of the Last Supper*, Salvador Dali (National Gallery of Art, Washington DC)

❖ *Last Supper*, Leonardo da Vinci (Convent of Sta. Maria delle Grazie, Milan)

❖ *Christ before Pilate*, Tintoretto (Scuola Grande di San Rocco, Venice)

❖ *Ecce Homo*, Antonio Ciseri (Galleria d'Arte Moderna, Florence)

❖ *Yellow Crucifixion*, Marc Chagall (Centre National d'Art et de Culture Georges Pompidou, Paris)

❖ *Crucifixion*, Tintoretto (Scuola Grande di San Rocco, Venice)

❖ *The Supper at Emmaus*, Caravaggio (National Gallery, London)

❖ *Doubting Thomas*, Caravaggio (Sanssouci Bilder-galerie, Potsdam)

❖ *Ascension*, Giotto di Bondone (Arena Chapel, Padua)

❖ *The Ascension*, Tintoretto (Scuola Grande di San Rocco, Venice)

See also *The Life of Jesus through the Eyes of an Artist*,
Paul Forsey (Barnabas) for images of:
Jesus washes the feet of his disciples
The Lord's supper
Jesus is arrested
Pilate questions Jesus
Jesus is nailed to a cross
Jesus is alive
Jesus and Thomas
The coming of the Holy Spirit

A CD-ROM of the images is free with the book and is also available separately for £4.99 (inc. VAT).

Music

✣ Messe Basse from *Missa Brevis* (Fauré)

✣ 'Mary, did you know?' from *Pure* (special edition, 2004) (Hayley Westenra)

✣ *Jesus Christ Superstar* (Rice/Lloyd Webber). Suitable tracks include:
   Hosanna
   The Last Supper
   Gethsemane (I only want to say)
   Trial by Pilate
   Crucifixion
   John 19:41

✣ Holy City from *Voices from Heaven* (Soweto Gospel Choir)

✣ *Dominus Jesus in Qua Nocte* (Palestrina)

✣ *St Matthew Passion* (J.S. Bach). Suitable tracks include:
   Behold, my Saviour now is taken
   O man bemoan thy grievous sin
   How falsely doth the world accuse
   To witness false my Saviour answ'reth not

✣ *The Crucifixion* (John Stainer). Suitable tracks include:
   And they came to a place named Gethsemane
   The agony
   Jesus said, 'Father, forgive them!'

✣ *The Armed Man* (Karl Jenkins). Suitable tracks include:
   Agnus Dei
   Benedictus
   Sanctus

✣ *Messiah* (G.F. Handel). Suitable tracks include:
   Thy rebuke hath broken his heart!
   Behold, and see if there be any sorrow
   I know that my Redeemer liveth
   Hallelujah Chorus

✣ Out of the deep from *Requiem* (John Rutter).

✣ *Go forth into the world in peace* (John Rutter)

✣ *O be joyful in the Lord* (John Rutter)

✤ The White Rider from *The Lord of the Rings: The Two Towers* (Howard Shore)
✤ *The Lord of the Rings: The Return of the King* (Howard Shore). Suitable tracks include:
  The Grey Havens
  Into the West
✤ *Jesu, joy of man's desiring* (J.S. Bach)
✤ *O how glorious is the kingdom* (Basil Harwood)
✤ *Te Deum* (Charpentier)
✤ *Te Deum* (Arvo Pärt)

Bible index